Business Environment

Business Environment

ASHISH BHALLA

B.Com, M.B.A. (Finance & Marketing)

Lecturer

Nikhil Institute of Engineering & Management, Agra.

VEI

AN ISO 9001:2008 CERTIFIED COMPANY

VAYU EDUCATION OF INDIA

2/25, Ansari Road, Darya Ganj, New Delhi-110 002

Business Environment

ISBN: 978-93-80712-88-8

First Edition: 2011

Reprint Edition: 2014

Price: ₹ 110.00

Printed & bound in India

Published by:

AN ISO 9001:2008 CERTIFIED COMPANY

VAYU EDUCATION OF INDIA

2/25, Ansari Road, Darya Ganj, New Delhi-110 002

Ph.: 91-11-47236600, 41564445

Fax: 91-11-41564440

E-mail: vei@veiindia.com

Web: www.veiindia.com

PREFACE

Organisations will have to formulate new growth strategies for success, expansion and increasing gains based on the day-to-day developments and the fast-moving worked. The need of the hour is to learn all the new policies, structures, measures, steps and the implications with reference to legal framework, foreign investment, privatisations, corporate governance and social responsibility, gaining knowledge about all these spectrums of business would help one to be a successful manager in the era of ever-increasing competition.

It is because of the importance of these topics and changing environment that universities and institutes have introduced Business Environment as a core subject in managemnt, commerce and economics streams. In some institutes this course has been covered under the titles like Economic Environment and Policies, Economic and Social Environment, Indian Economy, Developments in Indian and Global Economy, etc.

This book has been written in accordance with those MBA, M.Com., BBA and B.Com. outlined in the University Grants Commission Curriculum and will cater to the requirements of students.

ASHISH BHALLA

ACKNOWLEDGEMENT

Gratitude is the hardest of emotion to express and often does not find adequate words to convey that entire one feels, although it is difficult to mention the name of all, who gave me their full support and cooperation throughout my work.

There are numerous words in the English Dictionary but there is only one little magic word "thanks" which can replace all the other words and I have got hold of that word to thank to my Book.

We are specially thankful to Dr. Rajiv Kumar Jain, Managing Director, of Vayu Education of India, Darya Ganj, New Delhi-110002. Also thanks to Mr. Vijay Kumar Saini Production Manager, and other production team members of Vayu Education of India, published our book within a quite short duration in order to deliver a good quality book for the students who will really be benefited when they go through this book.

I am thankful to God who helped me. I dedicate this Book to my Father and Mother who has supported me at all the hard times.

ASHISH BHALLA

SYLLABUS

BUSINESS ENVIRONMENT

MBA-021

Unit I

The concept of Business Environment, significance and nature. Environment Scanning: Meaning, nature and scope, the process of environmental scanning, Interaction between internal and external environments, basic phailosophies of Capitalism and Socialism with their variants. Concepts of Mixed Economy.

Unit II

Overview of Political, Socio-cultureal, Legal, Technological and Global environment: An introduction to MRTP, FEMA, SEBI Act, Consumer Protection Act; The changing demesions of these laws and their impact on business.

Unit III

Philosophy and strategy of planning in India: Industrial Policy in recent years; Policy with regard to small scale industries; the monetary policy and fiscal policy, Stock Exchange-BSE-NSE. Depository system in India (Options, Futures and Derivatives) RBI-Role and functions, banking structure reforms; Narasimhan Committee Recommendations, Financial Sector reforms.

Unit IV

E-Banking in India-objectives, trends and practical uses-Recent technological developments in Indian Banking (ATM, Debit and Credit Cards, EMI, EFT) Cnsumerism, Social Responsibility of business enterprises, New Economic Policy, Globalistation, EXIM policy, FDI policy, Multinational Corporation (MNCs) and Transnational Corporations (TNCs)

CONTENTS

UNIT-I

Introduction to Business Environment 1-14

1.1 FEATURES OF BUSINESS ENVIRONMENT 1

1.2 IMPORTANCE OF BUSINESS ENVIRONMENT 2

1.3 ENVIRONMENTAL SCANNING/ANALYSIS 3
1.3.1 Process of Environmental Scanning/Analysis 3
1.3.2 Features of Environmental Scanning/Analysis 4
1.3.3 Factors Effecting the Environmental Scanning/Analysis 4
1.3.4 Uses/Significance/Utility/Benefit of Environmental Scanning/Analysis 6
1.3.5 Approaches of Environmental Scanning/Analysis 6

1.4 TYPES OF ENVIRONMENT 7
1.4.1 Internal Environment 7
1.4.2 External Environment 8
1.4.3 Types of External Environment 8

1.5 CAPITALISM ECONOMY 10
1.5.1 Features of Capitalism Economy 10
1.5.2 Advantages of the Capitalism 11
1.5.3 Disadvantages of the Capitalism Economy 11

1.6 SOCIALISM ECONOMY 12
1.6.1 Features of Socialism Economy 12
1.6.2 Advantages of the Socialism Economy 12
1.6.3 Disadvantages of the Socialism Economy 12

1.7 MIXED ECONOMY SYSTEM 13
1.7.1 Features of Mixed Economy 13

UNIT-II

Political Environment 15-30

2.1 POLITICAL ENVIRONMENT 15
2.1.1 Types of Political Systems 15

2.1.2 Economic Roles (or) Relationship of Government in Business 16
2.1.3 Political Risks of Global Business 17

2.2 SOCIO-CULTURAL ENVIRONMENT 18
2.2.1 Important factors influencing social environment 18
2.2.2 Culture Environment 19
2.2.3 Nature of Cultures 19
2.2.4 Impact of culture on business 19

2.3 TECHNOLOGICAL ENVIRONMENT 21
2.3.1 Features of Technology 21
2.3.2 Technological Environment in India 22
2.3.3 Positive Effect of Technological Environment 23

2.4 GLOBAL ENVIRONMENT 23
2.4.1 Essential Conditions for Global Environment 23
2.4.2 How to go global 24

2.5 MRTP ACT 24
2.5.1 Objectives of MRTP Act 1969 25
2.5.2 Criticism of MRTP Act 25

2.6 FOREIGN EXCHANGE MANAGEMENT ACT, 1999 26
2.6.1 Power to make regulations 27
2.6.2 Salient features of FEMA 27

2.7 SECURITIES AND EXCHANGE BOARD OF INDIA 28
2.7.1 Objectives of SEBI 28
2.7.2 Functions of SEBI 28
2.7.3 Powers of SEBI 29

2.8 CONSUMER PROTECTION ACT 1986 29
2.8.1 Rights of Consumers 29
2.8.2 Salient Feature of Consumer Protection Act 1986 30

UNIT-III

Planning in India 31-74

3.1 INTRODUCTION 31
3.1.1 Types of Planning 32
3.1.2 A Review of Five Year Plans 32
3.1.2.1 First Plan (1951-56) *32*
3.1.2.2 Second Plan (1956-61) *32*
3.1.2.3 Third Plan (1961-66) *33*
3.1.2.4 Fourth Plan (1969-74) *33*
3.1.2.5 Fifth Plan (1974-79) *33*
3.1.2.6 Sixth Plan (1980-85) *33*
3.1.2.7 Seventh Plan (1985-90) *34*
3.1.2.8 Eighth Plan (1992-97) *34*
3.1.2.9 Ninth Plan (1997-2002) *34*

3.1.2.10 Tenth Plan (2002-07) ... 35
3.1.3 Features of Tenth Plan ... 35
3.1.4 Approach Paper to 11th Plan ... 36
3.1.5 Changing nature of Planning ... 37

3.2 INDUSTRIAL POLICY ... 37
3.2.1 Rational for the industrial policy ... 38
3.2.2 Industrial Policy Resolution of 1948 ... 38
3.2.3 Industrial Policy Resolution of 1956 ... 40
3.2.4 Industrial Policy Resolution of February 2, 1973 ... 43
3.2.5 Industrial Policy resolution of December 23, 1977 ... 43
3.2.6 Industrial Policy Resolution of July 1980 ... 44
3.2.7 Industrial Policy Resolution of 1991 ... 44

3.3 SMALL-SCALE INDUSTRY ... 47
3.3.1 Measures of Small-Scale Units ... 48
3.3.2 Role of Small-Scale Industries in Indian Economy ... 48
3.3.3 Problems of SSI ... 49

3.4 MONETARY POLICY ... 50
3.4.1 Type of Monetary Policy ... 51
3.4.1 Objectives of Monetary Policy ... 51
3.4.3 Effectiveness of Monetary Policy ... 51
3.4.4 Instrument of Monetary Policy ... 52
3.4.5 Limitations of Monetary Policy ... 53

3.5 FISCAL POLICY ... 53
3.5.1 Objectives of Fiscal Policy ... 54
3.5.2 Fiscal Policy And Macroeconomic Goals ... 54
3.5.3 Instruments of Fiscal Policy ... 54
3.5.4 Economic effects of Fiscal Policy ... 55

3.6 STOCK EXCHANGE ... 55
3.6.1 Meaning and Definition of Stock Exchange ... 56
3.6.2 Role and importance of Stock Exchange ... 56
3.6.3 Functions of Stock Exchange ... 57
3.6.4 Services of Stock Exchange ... 57
3.6.5 Organisation Structure of Stock Exchange ... 58

3.7 BOMBAY STOCK EXCHANGE ... 58
3.7.1 About the Bombay Stock Exchange ... 59

3.8 NATIONAL STOCK EXCHANGE OF INDIA ... 59
3.8.1 Objectives of National Stock Exchange ... 59
3.8.2 Features of NSE ... 60

3.9 CAPITAL MARKET ... 60
3.9.1 Security Definition ... 60
3.9.2 Functions of Capital Market ... 61
3.9.3 Features of Indian Capital Market ... 61
3.9.4 Capital Market Structure ... 62

3.10 MONEY MARKET 63
3.10.1 Features of a Money Market 63
3.10.2 Objectives of Money Market 64
3.10.3 Structure of Indian Money Market 64
3.10.4 Components of Money Market 64
3.11 DEPOSITORY SYSTEM IN INDIA 66
3.11.1 Key Features of the Depository System in India 66
3.11.2 Options 67
3.11.3 Types of Options 67
3.11.4 Futures 68
3.11.5 Characteristics of Derivatives 68
3.11.6 Product, Participants and Functions of Derivatives 68
3.11.7 Types of Derivatives 69
3.12 RESERVE BANK OF INDIA 70
3.12.1 Necessity of a Central Bank 70
3.12.2 Principal of Central Bank 70
3.12.3 Function of Central bank 71
3.13 BANKING SECTOR REFORMS 71
3.14 NARASIMHAN COMMITTEE 73
3.15 FINANCIAL SECTOR REFORM IN INDIA 73

UNIT-IV

E-Banking 75-113
4.1 DEFINITION OF E-BANKING 75
4.1.1 Various Form of E-Banking 76
4.1.2 Benefits of E-Banking 78
4.1.3 Concerns with E-Banking 79
4.1.4 The Indian Experience of E-banking 79
4.2 CONSUMERISM 81
4.2.1 Consumer Rights 81
4.2.2 Utility of Consumerism 81
4.2.3 Consumer Protection 82
4.2.4 Consumer Protection and Consumerism in India 82
4.3 SOCIAL RESPONSIBILITY OF BUSINESS 83
4.3.1 Factors affecting Social Responsibility of Business Enterprise 83
4.3.2 Arguments for Social Responsibility 83
4.3.3 Arguments against Social Responsibility 84
4.3.4 Social Responsibilities towards different sections 84
4.4 NEW ECONOMIC POLICY-1991 85
4.4.1 Features of the new policy 85
4.4.2 Components of New Economic policy 85
4.4.3 Outcome of New Economic policy 86

4.4.3.1 Liberalization *86*
4.4.3.2 Privatization *87*
4.5 GLOBALISATION 88
4.5.1 Parameter of Globalisation 88
4.5.2 Features of Globalisation 88
4.5.3 Sources of Globalisation 88
4.5.4 Advantages of Globalization 89
4.5.5 Disadvantages of Globalization 89
4.5.6 Process of Globalisation 89
4.5.7 Essential Condition of Globalisation 89
4.5.8 Types/Components of Globalisation 90
4.5.9 Methods of Globalisation of Technology 91
4.5.10 Reasons for Globalisation of Investments 92
4.6 EXIM POLICY 92
4.6.1 Objectives of EXIM Policy 92
4.6.2 EXIM Policy (1992-1997) 92
4.6.3 EXIM Policy (1997-2002) 93
4.6.4 EXIM Policy (1999-2000) 94
4.6.5 EXIM Policy (2000-2001) 94
4.6.6 EXIM Policy, 2001-2002 96
4.6.7 EXIM Policy (2002-2007) 96
4.6.8. EXIM Policy (2003-2004) 98
4.6.9 EXIM Policy of India (2004-09) 98
4.7 FOREIGN DIRECT INVESTMENT 100
4.7.1 Types of FDI 100
4.7.2 Features of FDI 101
4.7.3 Factors Influencing FDI 104
4.7.4 FDI in India 106
4.7.5 Advantages of FDI 108
4.7.6 Prohibited Sectors for FDI 109
4.8 FOREIGN INSTITUTIONAL INVESTOR 109
4.8.1 Parameters on which SEBI decides FII applicants' eligibility 109
4.8.2 Advantages of FII 109
4.8.3 Disadvantages of FII 110
4.9 MULTINATIONAL CORPORATIONS 110
4.9.1 Organization of Multinational Corporations 111
4.9.2 Reasons for the Growth of MNC's 111
4.9.3 Merits of MNC's 111
4.9.4 Demerits of MNC's 112
4.9.5 Multinationals in India 112

Multiple Choice Questions 115-122
Index 123-125

UNIT- 1

Introduction to Business Environment

The formula for business success requires two elements – the individual and the environment. Remove either value and success becomes impossible. Business environment consist of all those factors that have a bearing on the business.

The term Business environment implies those external forces factors and institutions that are beyond the control of individual business organisations and their management and affect the business enterprise. It implies all external forces within which a business enterprise operates.

Business environment influence the functioning of the business system. Thus, business environment may be defined as all those conditions and forces which are external to the business and are beyond the individual business unit, but it operates within it. These forces are customer, creditors, competitors, government, socio-cultural organisations, political parties national and international organisations etc. some of those forces affect the business directly which some others have indirect effect on the business.

Business Environment has been defined by

Bayard O. Wheeler as "the total of all things external to firms and industries which affect their organization and operation".

According to Arthur M. Weimer, business environment encompasses the 'climate' or set of conditions, economic, social, political or institutional in which business operations are conducted.

1.1 FEATURES OF BUSINESS ENVIRONMENT

On the basis of the above discussion the features of business environment can be summarised as follows.

1. Business environment is the sum total of all factors external to the business firm and that greatly influences their functioning.
2. It covers factors and forces like customers, competitors, suppliers, government, and the social, cultural, political, technological and legal conditions.
3. The business environment is dynamic in nature that means it keeps on changing.
4. The changes in business environment are unpredictable. It is very difficult to predict the exact nature of future happenings and the changes in economic and social environment.
5. Business Environment differs from place to place, region to region and country to country. Political conditions in India differ from those in Pakistan. Taste and values cherished by people in India and China vary considerably.

1.2 IMPORTANCE OF BUSINESS ENVIRONMENT

There is a close and continuous interaction between the business and its environment. This interaction helps in strengthening the business firm and using its resources more effectively.

As stated above, the business environment is multifaceted, complex, and dynamic in nature and has a far-reaching impact on the survival and growth of the business. To be more specific, proper understanding of the social, political, legal and economic environment helps the business in the following ways:

1. **Determining Opportunities and Threats:** The interaction between the business and its environment would identify opportunities for and threats to the business. It helps the business enterprises for meeting the challenges successfully.
2. **Giving Direction for Growth:** The interaction with the environment leads to opening up new frontiers of growth for the business firms. It enables the business to identify the areas for growth and expansion of their activities.
3. **Continuous Learning:** Environmental analysis makes the task of managers easier in dealing with business challenges. The managers are motivated to continuously update their knowledge, understanding and skills to meet the predicted changes in realm of business.
4. **Image Building:** Environmental understanding helps the business organisations in improving their image by showing their sensitivity to the environment within which they are working. For example, in view of the shortage of power, many companies have set up Captive Power Plants (CPP) in their factories to meet their own requirement of power.
5. **Meeting Competition:** It helps the firms to analyse the competitors' strategies and formulate their own strategies accordingly.
6. **Identifying Firm's Strength and Weakness:** Business environment helps to identify the individual strengths and weaknesses in view of the technological and global developments.

1.3 ENVIRONMENTAL SCANNING/ANALYSIS

It is a process by which managers monitors the economic, governmental, technological, legal, social and cultural factors to determine the threats to the organization and the opportunities available to the organization. Environmental Scanning or Analysis is important in evaluating the present strategy, setting strategic objectives and formulating future strategies.

Mismatch between organization and its environment is the major cause of corporate decline. Companies must be sensitive towards environment factors which help them to change in advance regarding the change required by the organization from time to time.

SWOT ANALYSIS:

S = Strength

W = Weakness

O = Opportunities

T = Threats

Definition of SWOT

"Opportunity and threats are the external to the organization whose internal Strength and Weakness are decisive factors whether or not environment can be properly managed or not. With Strengths, an organization can seize the opportunities and capitalize on it, and because of its weakness, it becomes the victim of threat in the environment"

Need of Environmental Analysis

1. It is being conducted to create the understanding of current and potential change taking place in the environment.
2. To gather the information for strategic decision making.
3. Development of action plan to deal with technological advancement
4. To keep oneself dynamic.
5. It helps to understand the transformation of industrial environment.
6. It helps in identification of risk (cultural, social competitor, management, natural exchange rate).
7. It is a pre requisite for the formulation of right strategies.
8. It makes the managers aware of the organisation-environment linkage.

1.3.1 Process of Environmental Scanning/Analysis

Environmental scanning is a process and includes some specific steps. Those steps are:

1. **Preparing groundwork for scanning:** Organization try to understand why the changes are taking place in the economy and for that, organization look into the past records and come to the conclusion purely on the basis of historical data.

2. **Estimating future business:** On the basis of past records the future business is projected but the organization just use these projections as guidelines and not the absolute truth.
3. **Comparing actual with projected results:** At the time of actual changes, organization compares the actual impact of those changes with its projected results to identify any deviation. And if there is any deviation then organization can take the corrective actions as soon as possible.
4. **Refining the scanning/forecasting process:** As the scanning/forecasting is a continuous process, if company lacks in doing an effective scanning, then next time it will try to scan the environment in more effective way to minimize deviations.

1.3.2 Features of Environmental Scanning/Analysis

- **Continuous Process**: The Environmental Scanning is a continuous process.
- **Exploratory Process**: Choosing the alternatives available for future.
- **Holistic Exercise**: Organization must scan the whole environment in order to minimize the chance of surprise and maximize its utilities as an early warning system.

1.3.3 Factors Effecting the Environmental Scanning/Analysis

1. **Individual Factor:** The individual factors identified as influencing the scanning activity were information consciousness and exposure to information.

   Information consciousness means the attitude towards information-related activities, denoting the value attributed to information. This category emerged in the course of the analysis process, as a result of grouping together events, and the concepts describing them, which were judged as pertaining to the same category of events. Those concepts included the personal sense of responsibility for environmental scanning and the communication pattern developed by the individual. All the interviewees agreed about the vital role of information in business. Top managers of large and medium-size companies operating in different sub-sectors described their role, as far as environmental scanning is concerned, as a mix of personal monitoring and dissemination of information among direct collaborators.

   Communication among managers was made up of a mix of oral information and written information; the nature of this mix and the reasons that determine the choice of either of the forms of communication was not entirely clarified. However, some interviewees associated the choice of oral communication with the generic scope of the information or its potential for starting action.

   Exposure to information means the frequency of opportunities of contact with well-informed people and information-rich contexts. The emergence of this category was based on the analysis of the information networks developed by managers. All the interviewees played a very similar role, since they were all managers, either chief executives or entrepreneurs, or functional directors, mainly marketing and commercial directors. They were therefore in a privileged position concerning the degree of exposure to information.

Exposure to information is strongly influenced by the 'outwardness' of the organization: some organizations provide more opportunities of contact with well informed people or information-rich contexts. It is also influenced by the role played by the individual within the organization: marketing and commercial directors have a much greater exposure to information than financial or administrative directors. But exposure to information is also influenced by the information climate of the organizations, which differ in the range of conditions of access to and use of information by their staff.

2. **Organizational Factor:** The organizational factors identified as influencing the environmental scanning activity were information climate and outwardness.

   The information climate means the setting of conditions that determine access to and use of information in an organization. It was assessed through the information infrastructure implemented, i.e., the processes, technologies and people used in information acquisition and handling (collecting, organizing and making information available, and disseminating it). But it was the emergence of evidence relating to the role of organizational culture in shaping the information infrastructure that led to the creation of the construct "information climate".

   Organizational culture emerged as an important factor in the analysis of information issues within these organizations. The type of information culture that prevails in the pharmaceutical companies analyzed is a formal information culture, meaning cultures "which exhibit extensive formalization and systematization of information channels", as defined by Brown (1990).

   Two other companies in two different sub-sectors were identified as having, respectively, an oral culture, meaning cultures "which support a high degree of word-of-mouth communication", according to Brown (op. cit.) and an information conscious culture (cultures "which demonstrate considerable awareness of the value of information and sophistication in their information behaviour and systems", still according to Brown, 1990). No kind of information culture had developed in the remaining companies, where there was little sensitiveness to information matters, and little investment was made in the information infrastructure.

   Besides those two main relationships or connections, represented in the figure above by thick arrows, there are indications (represented by broken arrows) that managers with a strong information consciousness tend to foster their organizations' outwardness; on the other hand, where a stimulating information climate is created, the individual exposure to information increases.

As a result of the qualitative analysis of evidence from companies in the chemical industries sector in Portugal, we have evolved four theoretical concepts and have proposed relationships among them. The concepts relate to both organizational and individual behaviour. We suggest that, in terms of information-seeking to support organizational functions, both sets of factors must be taken into account. Further, we propose that the more open the organization is to its environment, particularly in terms of openness to information flows, the more likely it is that individuals in the organization will experience exposure to relevant information and develop an information consciousness. Similarly, to the extent that this occurs, the organization is more likely to develop an information climate that supports the individual.

1.3.4 Uses/Significance/Utility/Benefit of Environmental Scanning/Analysis

- To know the socio-economic changes at the national and international levels.
- To make the strategies and long-term policies for organization.
- To know the competitor's business strategies.
- To understand the transformation of the industry environment.
- To anticipate the present and future opportunities and threats.
- To develop action plans to deal the technological changes.
- To become dynamic for the organizational environment.

1.3.5 Approaches of Environmental Scanning/Analysis

Approaches mean gathering, collecting or intake of essential information which are required for Environmental Scanning. These Approaches are:-

1. **Systematic Approach:** Under this those information for environment scanning are collected which have a direct impact on an organization's activities such as:
   - Change in regulations
   - Markets
   - Customers
   - Govt. policies.

Information regarding these should be collected regular basis to monitor changes and to take corrective actions in time.

2. **Adhoc Approach:** Under this approach information for environmental scanning are not collected regularly but organization do special surveys or studies or investigations for some special projects at the time of requirement to identify the unforeseen developments and changes in the economic environment.
3. **Processed-Form Approach:** Information is collected through primary or secondary sources:

- **Primary Sources:** Direct from Government
- **Secondary Sources:** Newspapers, magazines, periodicals etc.

1.4 TYPES OF ENVIRONMENT

On the basis of the extent of intimacy with the firm, the environmental factors may be classified into different types-internal and external.

1.4.1 Internal Environment

The internal environment is the environment that has a direct impact on the business. Here there are some internal factors which are generally controllable because the company has control over these factors. It can alter or modify such factors as its personnel, physical facilities, and organization and functional means, like marketing, to suit the environment.

The important internal factors which have a bearing on the strategy and other decisions of internal organization are discussed below.

Value system

The value system of the founders and those at the helm of affairs has important bearing on the choice of business, the mission and the objectives of the organization, business policies and practices.

Mission and vision and objectives

Vision means the ability to think about the future with imagination and wisdom. Vision is an important factor in achieving the objectives of the organization. The mission is the medium through which the objectives are achieved.

Management structure and nature

The structure of the organization also influences the business decisions. The organizational structure like the composition of board of directors influences the decisions of business as they are internal factors. The structure and style of the organization may delay a decision making or some other helps in making quick decisions.

Internal power relationships

The relationship among the three levels of the organization also influences on the business. The mutual co-ordination among those three is an important need for a business. The relationship among the people working in the three levels of the organization should be cordial.

Human Resource

The human resource is the important factor for any organization as it contributes to the strength and weakness of any organization. the human resource in any organization must have characteristics like skills, quality, high morale, commitment towards the work , attitude, etc. T he involvement and initiative of the people in an organization at different levels may vary from organization to organization. The organizational culture and overall environment have bearing on them.

Company Image and Brand Equity

The image of the company in the outside market has the impact on the internal environment of the company. It helps in raising the finance, making joint ventures other alliances, expansions and acquisitions, entering sale and purchase contracts, launching new products, etc. Brand equity also helps the company in same way.

1.4.2 External Environment

It refers to the environment that has an indirect influence on the business. The factors are uncontrollable by the business. There are two types of external environment.

1.4.3 Types of External Environment

Micro Environment

The micro environment is also known as the task environment and operating environment because the micro environmental forces have a direct bearing on the operations of the firm.

"The micro environment consists of the actors in the company's immediate environment that affects the performance of the company. These include the suppliers, marketing intermediaries, competitors, customers and the public"

The micro environmental factors are more intimately linked with the company than the macro factors. The micro forces need not necessarily affect all the firms in a particular industry in the same way. Some of the micro factors may be particular to a firm. When the competing firms in an industry have the same micro elements, the relative success of the firms depends on their relative effectiveness in dealing with these elements.

Suppliers

An important force in the micro environment of a company is the suppliers, i.e., those who supply the inputs like raw materials and components to the company. The importance of reliable source/sources of supply to the smooth functioning of the business is obvious.

Customer

The major task of a business is to create and sustain customers. A business exists only because of its customers. The choice of customer segments should be made by considering a number of factors including the relative profitability, dependability, and stability of demand, growth prospects and the extent of competition.

Competition

Competition not only include the other firms that produce same product but also those firms which compete for the income of the consumers the competition here among these products may be said as desire competition as the primary task here is to fulfil the desire of the customers. The competition that satisfies a particular category desire then it is called generic competition.

Marketing Intermediaries

The marketing intermediaries include middlemen such as agents and merchants that help the company find customers or close sales with them. The marketing intermediaries are vital links between the company and the final consumers.

Financiers

The financiers are also important factors of internal environment. Along with financing capabilities of the company their policies and strategies, attitudes towards risk, ability to provide non-financial assistance etc. are very important.

Public

Public can be said as any group that has an actual or potential interest in or on an organization's ability to achieve its interest. Public include media and citizens. Growth of consumer public is an important development affecting business.

Macro Environment

Macro environment is also known as General environment and remote environment. Macro factors are generally more uncontrollable than micro environment factors. When the macro factors become uncontrollable , the success of company depends upon its adaptability to the environment. Some of the macro environment factors are discussed below:

Economic Environment

Economic environment refers to the aggregate of the nature of economic system of the country, business cycles, the socio-economic infrastructure etc. The successful businessman visualizes the external factors affecting the business, anticipating prospective market situations and makes suitable to get the maximum with minimize cost.

Social Environment

The social dimension or environment of a nation determines the value system of the society which, in turn affects the functioning of the business. Sociological factors such as costs structure, customs and conventions, mobility of labour etc. have far-reaching impact on the business. These factors determine the work culture and mobility of labour, work groups etc.

Political Environment

The political environment of a country is influenced by the political organisations such as philosophy of political parties, ideology of government or party in power, nature and extent of bureaucracy influence of primary groups etc. . The political environment of the country influences the business to a great extent.

Legal Environment

Legal environment includes flexibility and adaptability of law and other legal rules governing the business. It may include the exact rulings and decision of the courts. These affect the business and its managers to a great extent.

Technical Environment

The business in a country is greatly influenced by the technological development. The technology adopted by the industries determines the type and quality of goods and services to be produced and the type and quality of plant and equipment to be used. Technological environment influences the business in terms of investment in technology, consistent application of technology and the effects of technology on markets.

Economic Systems

It refers to the extent of govt. regulation and intervention in the areas of employment, income distribution, consumption, competition, saving, investment etc. in the economy. The arrangement of market distribution of goods and services earning of people and standard of living highly affected by the role of the government in the economy.

1.5 CAPITALISM ECONOMY

In a market capitalist system, capital and land are private property. Enterprises may be formed by individuals who can get access to land and equipment, either because they own it or can rent or borrow to get it, and who can hire labour or employ themselves. Enterprises organize and direct production, and they are operated for the private benefit of the person who organizes the enterprise. Private benefit is interpreted as profit, so we say that the enterprises maximize profits.

In a capitalist economy, production is limited by existing resources, technology and profit which are privately owned rather than property rights held by the government on behalf of society. And it makes sense that an economic system based on profit would produce any given product or service. In this kind of system, most allocate decision is coordinated by the consumers and producers.

1.5.1 Features of Capitalism Economy

1. **Private ownership:** The factors of production such as land, labour, capital are privately owned and the production progresses at private initiative.
2. **Free enterprise:** Private firms are allowed to obtain resources to organize production and to sell the output in any way they want.
3. **Consumer Sovereignty:** It implies "Consumer is the king". The production decision are based on consumer desires and is reflected is the demand pattern.
4. **Freedom of choice of occupation:** In the capitalist economy the individual is free to choose any job as per his qualification, but this system does not ensure a job security.

5. **Freedom to save and invest:** In a capitalist system the individuals are free to save, invest and accumulate wealth through investment. Thus in such a system people save their money for future consumption.
6. **Market System:** In a capitalist economy the buyers and sellers express their opinions about how much they are willing to pay and how much they demand for goods.
7. **Competition:** In a capitalist economy high degree of competition reduces market imperfections. Competition is necessary to keep initiative constantly on assets, to protect the consumer and to maintain a flexible price system.
8. **Absence of a central plan:** The activities of the numerous economic units are not controlled and regulated by the govt. There is an absence of central regulatory plan. Everybody is free to do whatever it likes.
9. **Limited Role of govt:** The absence of a central plan does not imply that the govt. Is not playing any role. Govt. intervention is necessary to ensure the protection of the property rights, enforce contractual agreements, taxation and other community wants. However the role is very much limited.

1.5.2 Advantages of the Capitalism

There are a few of the advantages of the capitalism Economy.

1. Capacity to achieve economic efficiency as a result of the lowest cost of the production being force by the competition and profit motive.
2. It creates a freedom economic. Consumers, producers and workers are free to make their own decisions based on their own interest. Capitalistic economies allow a worker's excellence to be rewarded either by money or by position. Capitalism is also a system that promotes creativity and inventiveness on the part of the workers.

1.5.3 Disadvantages of the Capitalism Economy

There are a few of the disadvantages of the capitalism.

1. Capitalism also has its own disadvantages which creates an unequal distribution of income. Which mean gap between higher and the lower income are very obvious.
2. Secondly, capitalism brings harms to the environment as a result of pursuit for more profits.
3. And the Third disadvantage is where in the early form of capitalism was proprietary capitalism. One problem for proprietary capitalism is that these individual enterprises seldom got very large. This meant that many projects that could have been useful and profitable could not be undertaken by capitalist firms, because the projects were too large to afford them.

   As an example there are only a few nation has been classified as capitalist nation such as United States, Japan, Canada and Hong Kong.

1.6 SOCIALISM ECONOMY

Socialism can be defined as an economic system which has been characterized by the government ownership of recourses and centralized decision making. Under a socialist economic system, individuals own their own human capital and the government owns most other, non-human resources, most of the major factors of production are owned by the state. Land, factories, and major machinery are publicly owned.

A socialist system is a form of command economy in which prices and production are set by the state. Resources can only move at the direction of the centralized planning authority. Economic decisions are all made by the state through its central planning agencies. Socialism is an economic system based upon the individual's good will toward others, rather than a function of his or her own self-interest. In socialism, individuals are urged to consider the well-being of others; if individuals don't behave in a socially desirable manner, the government will intervene. Socialism has become an economic system based on government ownership of the means of production, with economic activity governed by centralize decision making.

1.6.1 Features of Socialism Economy

- Govt. ownership or control.
- Central authority.
- Restriction or consumption.
- Restrictions on occupation.
- Fixation of wages and prices
- Equitable distribution of income.

1.6.2 Advantages of the Socialism Economy

1. One of the advantages of the socialism is superior in achieving an equitable distribution of income because the government ownership of main recourses prevents a individuals or groups get a bigger income than other from the nation wealth.
2. Secondly, socialism will bring a rapid economic growth.

1.6.3 Disadvantages of the Socialism Economy

1. The main problem of a socialistic system is that there are no good examples of purely socialistic systems to use as examples or models for employing the theory in practice.
2. The State was the organization that controlled all the sectors of the economy and those in power, succeeded in abusing the population, except for the very elite of society. There is also no motivation for many workers to excel at their jobs because there is no benefit to the worker. Any benefits derived from a worker working hard would be equalized among all workers, therefore the driving force evaporates.

For example, Cuba and North Korea is one of the nations with a socialist economic system.

1.7 MIXED ECONOMY SYSTEM

In practice, most economies blend some elements of both market and command economies in answering the three fundamental economic questions: What and how much will be produced? How will it be produced? For whom will it be produced? Furthermore, within any economy, the degree of the mix will vary.

The economy of the United States is generally considered to be a free market or capitalist economic system. However, even in the United States the government has determined a minimum wage, has set rules and regulations for environmental protection, has provided price supports for agricultural products, restricts the imports of items that might compete with local production, restricts the exports of sensitive output, provides for public goods such as a park system, and provides health and retirement services through Medicaid and Medicare. All of these detract from the essential nature of a capitalist economy. However, most decisions continue to be left to free markets, leaving the United States as a mixed economy that leans heavily toward the capitalist economic system.

In contrast, the economy of the former Soviet Union is generally considered to be communist. However, the strict controls of the central planning unit of the country tended to be more intensely focused on heavy industry, including the defence and aerospace industries, than on agricultural industries. Farmers often had significant freedom to produce and sell (or barter) what they wished.

"Mixed Economy can be defined as a form of organization where the elements of both capitalist economy and socialist economy are found. This economy is adopted by India where there is Existence of both Public and Private sectors working together".

1.7.1 Features of Mixed Economy

1. **Co-existence of public and private sector:** In a mixed economy, both public and private sector plays the role is the economy. Also public and private sector combines to form joint sector. Usually same sensitive industries are under the role of govt. In such economies.
2. **Existence of competition:** The mixed economy is characterized by the extent of competition in certain areas where there is no Government monopoly, However Government acts as a watchdog of the market competition.
3. **Freedom on Consumption in selected areas :** In a mixed economy, consumer is the king in certain desired products and services while rest others are in the hands of state where the consumer don't have its choice neither in production nor in fixation of prices.
4. **Freedom to save and invest:** People are free to save the money as part of their earnings and they can invest this money in the desired areas. However the Government regulates almost each and every sector of the economy.

5. **Freedom of occupation:** In a mixed economy people are free to do the jobs as per their qualifications, skills, experience and interest. Government also provides employment to the people in the companies owned by it.
6. **Existence of central plan:** In a mixed economy though there is freedom to private sector in areas of production, selling and consumption but still the Government. has the authority of framing rules, regulations policies, laws and acts for each and every sector of the economy. If the individuals, bypass or infringe the govt. regulations then it calls for a punishment or penalty.
7. **Market Mechanism :** In a mixed economy, goods and services are produced according to the needs and preference of the customers. Both the buyers and the sellers has the bargaining power and the prices of commodities are fixed on the basis of the forces of demand and supply.
8. **Inequitable distribution of Income:** Mixed economies exhibit almost all the classes of people according to their income and consequently standard of living. Since there is a larger scope of employment and the wages and salaries are not fixed by the Government. So people have good earning at their disposal.

UNIT-2

Political Environment

2.1 POLITICAL ENVIRONMENT

This includes the political system, the government policies and attitude towards the business community and the unionism. All these aspects have a bearing on the strategies adopted by the business firms. The stability of the government also influences business and related activities to a great extent. It sends a signal of strength, confidence to various interest groups and investors.

2.1.1 Types of Political Systems

1. **Democracy:** Democracy is for the people, by the people, and of the people, it's similar to participative management, in this system people are encouraged to participate in decision making, a peoples representative can be selected by the people through a process of election, and the responsibility of leading the nation is kept on the shoulders of the elected representative. Eg. India
2. **Dictatorship:** It is also called as authoritarianism, which is quite opposite to democracy, here the hole power is in the hands of the leader, and people should follow the leader, all the policies related to economy, business etc are governed by the leader. Eg Saudi Arabia

Government Controls and Regulations

Regulating economic and industrial activities - Industrial Licensing policy - Control of monopolies - Capital issues control - Government control over FDI and collaboration - Distribution and price control – new EXIM policy - Foreign exchange flow regulation - Technology transfer.

In an economy, all the sectors of business will be functioning within the frame work of the rules and regulation of the country. All types of business owe their existence through the privileges guaranteed under the constitution of the country. The day-to-day working and the style of functioning of business in a country depend upon the economic policy of the government and the rules and regulation framed. The socio economic and political objectives of the government and the basic guiding principles of the state have been laid down preamble to the constitution, in the Fundamental rights and in Directive principles of the state. The Preamble to the Zambian constitutions is; Zambia is Democratic republic secure to all its citizens.

- JUSTICE, Social, economic and political
- LIBERTY of thought, expression, belief, faith and worship
- EQUALITY of status and opportunity; and to promote among them all
- FRATERNITY assuring the dignity of the individual and the unity and integrity of the Nation.

2.1.2 Economic Roles (or) Relationship of Government in Business

The Government is a very powerful institution which has a very important role in shaping the national economy. Almost all countries of the world have realized the need of government intervention in creating a favourable business environment. The government normally plays four important roles in an economy, for shaping the business environment. The nature and extent of the cited roles of the government will vary depending upon a given situation. They are as follows;

1. Government as a regulator of business
2. Government as a promoter of business
3. Government as an entrepreneur
4. Government as the Planner.

1. **Government as a regulator of business:** All regulatory policies of the government enacted the legislatures of the countries are covered by this segment. Government regulation of the business may cover a very wide spectrum, right from the entry of business to the final stage of the business units. Through licensing system, the government may regulate the entry of a firm into a particular line of business. The governments' regulatory measures on business may be either Direct control or Indirect control or with the combination of both.
    - **Direct control:** these are administrative physical controls with regards to trade and industry, by placing limits for expansion, control of monopoly, and big business, or starting public enterprise in place of private. These controls are applied selectively from firm to firm and industry to industry.
    - **Indirect control:** These are exercised by the government through several fiscal and monetary measures. By imposing penalties, adopting disincentive measures, extending incentives, subsidies, high import duty. The objective may be maintaining equilibrium in the allocation of resources or balanced regional development.
2. **Government as a promoter of business:** The promotional role of the government is very important in developing countries and also in developed countries. In developing

countries, there will be deplorable dearth of entrepreneurial skill and other infrastructural facilities. The government provides finance to industry, creating required minimum infrastructural facilities, providing subsidies and tax holidays. The government has to develop infrastructure such as power, transport, finance, marketing, institutions for training and guidance etc. And other promotional activities.

3. **Government as an entrepreneur:** In many countries government established its own industries and has to take entrepreneurial role the dearth of private entrepreneurship, unprofitable sectors or neglect of some sectors by the private business, absence of adequate competition and the resultant exploitation of consumers and socio-political ideologies of the state are all the contributing causes for the state to start the business and bear the risks. Generally, private investors are solely guided by profit motive and they will avert any enterprise involving high risks. Hence, they will not enter in areas of low returns and also public utility services where the investments are very heavy and the returns very meagre. The government does not hesitate to take them up as a 'Social responsibility'. Usually, capital intensive projects like steel, petroleum, fertilizers, and other capital goods industries where the investments would be very heavy and the gestation period too long, the government would setup its business.
4. **Government as the Planner:** The government is expected to bring about all-round prosperity. The government has to fulfil all the economics of the people and their aspirations. In its role as a planner, the government indicates the various priorities and makes sectoral allocations. The idea of economic planning can be traced to three different sources. They are:
   - **Rationalisation of Resources:** Since the resources of the economy are much limited, they have to be utilized in a rationalized way or in an optimal manner so as to achieve optimum satisfaction for the society. In other words, the planned economy is a rational economy which attempts to secure the maximum return with minimum wastage or productive resources.
   - **Socialisation of resources:** The planned economy helps in the realization of certain well defined social ends like economic equality, uniform growth etc. an unplanned economy, left to it, is incapable of attaining the desired social ends. The resources of the country should be will be possible only under social planning.
   - **Nationalisation of resources:** The concept connotes that a planned economy is a powerful economy. The nationalists want to use planning as a weapon to strengthen the country, not only economically, but also politically. This concept has a tinge of totalitarian principle.

2.1.3 Political Risks of Global Business

1. **Confiscation:** The most severe political risk is confiscation, which is seizing of company's assets without payment.

2. **Expropriation:** Which requires reimbursement, for the government seized investment.
3. **Domestication:** Which occurs when host country takes steps to transfer foreign investments to national control and ownership through series of government decrees? A change in the government's attitudes, policies, economic plans and philosophies toward the role of foreign investment is the reason behind the decision to confiscate, expropriate or domesticate existing foreign assets.

2.2 SOCIO-CULTURAL ENVIRONMENT

The society is that surrounded by the people they grow up their basic beliefs, values, and norms. Culture environment refers to the influence exercised by certain social factors which are 'beyond the company's gate' such factor include, among others, attitude of people to work, attitude to wealth, family, marriage, religion, education, and ethics.

Culture is the human-made part of the human environment - the sum total of mankind's knowledge, beliefs, art, morals, laws, customs and other capabilities and habits acquired by humans as members of society. It is the distinctive way of life of a group of people.

Humans essentially create their own cultural and social environment. Customs, practices and traditions for survival and development are passed down from one generation to the next. In this way, the members of a particular society become conditioned to accept certain "truths" about life around them. The increasingly competitive international business environment calls upon exporters to tailor or adapt their business approach to the culture and traditions of specific foreign markets. The inability or unwillingness to do so could become a serious obstacle to success.

In the context of the socio-cultural environment, there are a number of factors that you will need to consider. These are:

- Language
- Material culture
- Aesthetics
- Social organisation
- Religious beliefs, attitudes, values, space and time

Social Environment

"The social environment consists of factors related to human relationship and development, forms and functions of such relationship having a bearing on the business of an organisation".

2.2.1 Important factors influencing social environment

1. The demographic characteristics such as population, density and distribution, change in population and age composition, migration, and rural- urban mobility, income distribution.
2. The social concerns such as role in business in society, environment pollution, corruption, consumerism, use of mass media, etc.

3. Social attitudes and Values such as expectation of society from business, social customs, beliefs, rituals and practices, changing life style patterns, and materialism.
4. Family structure and Changes in it, attitude towards and within the family, and family values.
5. Role of women in society, position of children and adolescents in family and society.
6. Educational levels, awareness and consciousness of rights, and work ethics of members of society.

2.2.2 Culture Environment

Culture may be defined as the behaviour of man as a member of society. It is the habit acquired by belief, knowledge of arts, morals, law and custom. In short, it is the socially sanctioned behaviour of people.

According to John Dewey, ' culture' is existence of society. Culture denotes the habit of people in a particular society, their manner of talk, behaviour, following of certain customs, the type of food they eat and the manner of eating, the dress they wear, the association they nurture and persons they marry, etc.

2.2.3 Nature of Cultures

Culture includes several behavioural influencing factors shared by members of a society and passed through generations.

The following characteristics of culture are worth knowing:

- **Learned:** culture is not inherited or biologically based; it is acquired by learning and experience.
- **Shared:** peoples as members of a group, organization or society share culture; it is not specific.
- **Tran generational:** culture is passed on from one generation to the next.
- **Symbolic:** culture is based on the human capacity to symbolize or use one thing to represent another.
- **Adaptive:** culture is based on the human capacity to change or adapt, as opposed to the more genetically driven.

2.2.4 Impact of Culture on Business

1. **Culture creates people:** The concept of culture is great significance to business because it is the culture which generally determines the ethos of the people. It trains people along particular lines, tending to put a personality stamp upon them. Thus, we have Indians, Americans, Germans, British, and so on.
2. **Culture and globalization:** As business units go international, the need for understanding and appreciating cultural differences across various countries is essential.

Work motivation business goals, negotiating styles ,attitudes towards the development of business relationship, gift-giving customs, greeting significance of body gesture , meaning of colours and numbers, and the like vary from country to country.

3. **Cultures determine goods and services:** Culture broadly determines the type of goods and services a business should produce. The type of food people eat, the clothes they wear, the beverages they drink and the building materials they use to construct dwelling houses vary from culture to culture and from to time within the same culture. Business should realize these cultural differences and bring out products accordingly.

4.. **Language and culture:** The interface between language and culture is strong. There three thousands language across the world. There is no perfect equivalent in English for the word punya. Language can be either low context or high context. Low context language is direct but high context language carries multiple meanings with it. European languages are low context type. Asian languages are high context type.

5.. **Attitudes:** Attitudes are positive or negative evaluations that determine one's behaviour. Culture determines people's attitudes towards business. French culture lays emphasis on elegance, eclecticism and form. But Mexican culture is death oriented.

6.. **Collectivism and individualism:** The spirit of collectivism and individualism is related to such personnel aspects as employee morale, multiplicity of trade unions and intra union rivalries. It is said that world. The feeling of collectivism or individualism has its influence on employee morale, multiplicity of unions and inter-union rivalry.

7.. **Ambitious or complacent:** Culture makes a person to become ambitious or complacent.

8.. **Education:** The interface between business and education, though a recent phenomenon, is a significant one. For a long time there was a stand-off between business and higher education. Now the two have become closer. Impact of education on business is basically three-fold attract high wage industries, market potential is enhanced, type of advertising and packaging.

9.. **Family:** Family is a remarkable institution vested with several significant contributions. Joint family had several benefits to offer but sadly it is waning. Joint families are now being replaced by nuclear family.

10.. **Religion:** Religion refers to a specific and institutionalized set of beliefs and practices agreed upon by number of persons. People practice abnormal things in the name of religion. Though receipt and payment of interest are prohibited, profit sharing is allowed in Islam. Creation of wealth is not encouraged in Buddhism.

2.3 TECHNOLOGICAL ENVIRONMENT

Technological environment include the methods, techniques and approaches adopted for production of goods and services and its distribution. The varying technological environments of different countries affect the designing of products.

Technology is one of the important determinants of success of a firm as well as economic and social development of nation. It includes both hardware and software to solve problems and promote progress.

1. **Innovative drive of company:** The term innovation means introduction of new product, the use of new method of production. "The technical, industrial and commercial steps which leads to marketing of new products and to commercial use of new technical process and equipment"
2. **Customers Needs/Expectation:** Technological orientation and R&D effects of a company may also be influenced by the customer needs and expectation. In several cases the customer and the supplier have a collaborative relationship to develop the product or solutions. If the customers are highly demanding, companies would be compelled to be innovative.
3. **Demand conditions:** The size of demand influences the choice of the technology. The size of demand influences the choice of the technological scale. Fast growing trend of demand would encourage development of technology of large scale.
4. **Suppliers offering:** Many times technological changes are encouraged by the suppliers of a company, like a capital goods supplier etc.
5. **Competitive dynamics:** Competition compels the adoption of the best technology and constant endeavour to innovate.
6. **Substitutes:** Emergence of new substitutes or technological improvements or substitutes which alter technological change.
7. **Social forces:** Certain social forces like pretext against environment pollution or other ecological problems demand for eco-friendly products.
8. **Research organization:** The technological environment of business is enriched by researched organizations which develops new technologies and provide other technical inputs.
9. **Govt. Policy:** The govt. contributes to the development to the technology by its own direct involvement by establishing research organization and funding R & D. The govt. may encourage private R & D by various incentives.

2.3.1 Features of Technology

1. **Technology Brings Change:** Technology brings change in every walk of life, like the way we cook, the way we commute, the way we communicate etc. technology has brought lot of changes in business from barter system to e-business.

2. **Technology Reduces Time:** Technology has drastically reduced time between conceiving an idea and implementing that idea. The world has become a global village, which has no barriers by the invention of internet technologies which has reduced time of transferring information in no time.
3. **Technology Reduces Distance:** With the invention of advanced transportation systems which has reduced the time to travel e.g. by the invention of supersonic jets etc.
4. **Technology Improves Quality of Life:** The quality of life of people has definitely improved, the advancements of medical technology the life expectancy rate is increased and the control of various diseases is possible.

Benefits of Technology in Management Decision Making

The managerial decisions are of two types

- Structured or programmed decisions
- Un-structures or non-programmed decisions

Technology helps the manager to make decisions related to business in the following ways

1. **Decision Support System:** It is an information system which collects the information from various sources like government, customers and suppliers and global market and competitors and helps the manager to interact with the mathematical decision models to make decision.
2. **Group Decision Support System :**An expert system with set of hardware, software & procedures that support a group of people engaged in a decision-related meeting.
3. **Office Automation System:** An office automation system uses computers or networks to carry out various office operations.
4. **Transaction Processing System:** A system that handles the processing and tracking of transactions is called TPS.
5. **Management Information System:** MIS is a set of software tools that enables managers to gather, organize, & evaluate information about a workgroup, department or entire organization.
6. **Expert System:** Expert System is a specialized application that performs tasks that would normally be done by a human.

2.3.2 Technological Environment in India

The government has realized the importance of technology in development plan and has accorded high priority. The following measures have been taken by the government to develop indigenous technology and import technology from outside.

1. The government gives incentives and provides financial and other assistance to upgrade obsolete machines or technology.

2. Foreign collaborations for import of technology are given more importance.
3. The import of computers and modem technology is allowed at reduced rates of import duties.
4. The government wants bridge the technology gap and thereby improve the quality of output. In the long run it will help Indian companies to compete successfully in the domestic and international market.

2.3.3 Positive Effect of Technological Environment

- Increase productivity.
- Production of new & better goods of standardized quality
- Effective use of country's resources
- Basis of fast growth of the business.

2.4 GLOBAL ENVIRONMENT

Globalization is an attitude of mind – which views the entire world as a single market so that the corporate strategy is based on the dynamics of the global business environment. Globalization encompasses the following:

1. Expanding business globally
2. Giving up distinction between domestic and foreign market and developing global outlook of business.
3. To maximize profit
4. For growth

2.4.1 Essential Conditions for Global Environment

1. **Business freedom:** There should not be necessary govt. restriction like import restriction, foreign investments etc.
2. **Facilities:** Enterprise can develop globally from home country bare depends on facilities available like the infrastructural facilities.
3. **Govt. support:** Govt support can encourage globalization, like infrastructural facilities, R & D support, and financial market reforms.
4. **Resources:** It decides the ability of firm to globalize. Resourceful companies may find it easier to thrust ahead in global market. Resources include finance, R&D, company and grand image, HR etc.
5. **Competitiveness:** A firm may drive a competitive advantage from any one or more of the factors such as low costs and price, product quality, product differentiation, technology superiority, marketing strength etc.

2.4.2 How to go global

Important foreign market entry strategies–

1. **Exporting:** Exporting the most traditional mode of entering global market.
2. **Licensing & franchising:** It involves minimal commitment of resources and effort on the part of international marketer, are easy way of entering foreign markets. Finalizing is a form of licensing in which a parent company grants another independent entity the right to do business.
3. **Contract manufacturing:** a company doing international marketing contracts with firms in the foreign countries to manufacture the products while retaining the responsibility of marketing the product.
4. **Management contracting:** In this supplier brings together a package of skills that will provide an integrated service to clients without risk on owner.
5. **Wholly owned manufacturing facilities:** It provides the firm with complete control over production and quality. It does not have risk in the development.
6. **Assembly operations:** Assembly facilities in foreign markets are very ideal when there are economies of scale in the manufacture. When assembly operations are labour intensive and labour is cheap in foreign country.
7. **Joint ventures:** Joint venture is a very common strategy of entering foreign market. Any form of association which implies collaboration for more than a transitory period is a joint venture. A joint venture may bring about by a foreign investor buying an interest in a local company.
8. **Third country location:** Third country location is also an entry strategy, when there is no commercial transaction between two nations for some reasons, a firm in one of their nations which wants to enter the other market will have to operate third country base.
9. **Mergers and acquisitions:** It has very good market entry strategy as well as expansion strategy. It provides instant access to markets and distribution network.

2.5 MRTP ACT

The Principal Law in India to deal with competition was Monopolistic and Restrictive Trade Practices Act, 1969. The MRTP Act, brought into force form

1 June 1970, was a very controversial piece of legislation. The high level committee on Competition Policy and law, appointed by Government of India, recommended that a new competition. Act may be enacted and MRTP Act may be repeated.

The Government has accepted their recommendation. The MRTP Act, one of the most, controversial piece of legislation in India, has thus become a document of historical value. The salient features of this Act are given her because of the importance with which it rained the industrial sector of the country.

2.5.1 Objectives of MRTP Act 1969

The main objectives of MRTP Act 1969 were

1. Prevention of concentration of economic power to common detriment.
2. Control of Monopolistic, restrictive and unfair trade practices which are pre judicial to public interest.

The main thrust of the MRTP Act now is the achievement of Prevention of Monopolistic, restrictive and unfair trade practices. Thus, the 'M' las almost been knocked out of MRTP Act.

In other words, large companies have been freed from MRTPA requirement of prior permission of the government for substantial expansion of existing undertaking, eatables wing new undertakings and MEAs.

In accordance with the Provisions of the Act, the Government of India had set up a Commission known as the Monopolistic & Restrictive Trade Practices Commission.

The MRTP Commission was vested with Power to inquire into restrictive, monopolistic and unfair trade practices. The MRTP Act empowered the central Government to control and prohibit those monopolistic, restrictive & unfair trade practices that are, or are likely to be prejudicial to the public interest.

Monopolistic Trade Practice: is a trade practice which has, or is likely to have, the effect of unreasonably preventing or lessening competition in the production, supply or distribution of any goods or services, limiting technical development and capital investment to the common detriment or allowing quality of goods or services to deteriorate.

A Restrictive Trade Practice: is a trade practice which has the effect, actual or probable of restricting, lessening or destroying competition. Such trade practices may tend to obstruct the flow of production or to bring about manipulation of prices or condition of delivery etc, to the common detriment.

An Unfair trade Practice: is a trade practice which, for the purpose of promoting the sale, use or supply of any goods or the provision of any services, adopts one or more unfair trade practices (like misleading advertisements) & thereby causes loss or injury to the consumers of such goods or services, whether by eliminating or restricting competition or otherwise. The Act also empowered the commission to make any undertaking or person to pay compensation to the party who suffered a loss or damage as a result of unfair trade practice carried on by undertaking or person.

2.5.2 Criticism of MRTP Act

- Because of its defeating Provisions. We had a very situation of not allowing Indian companies to grow by capacity expansion, establishment of new units or by M&A an because of short supply importing goods produced by foreign multinationals which were far larger in size than the Indian biggies, spending the scarce foreign exchange.

- The MRTP Act, besides adversely affecting economic growth, blunted Indian Companies ability to grow, consolidate and improve competitiveness. This had had a very dampening effect on their global competitiveness.

2.6 FOREIGN EXCHANGE MANAGEMENT ACT, 1999

Upon review of the Foreign Exchange Regulation Act, 1973 (FERA) in 1993, it was realised that significant changes had taken place since the promulgation of FERA. Among the major changes noticed were: Large increase in country's Foreign Exchange Reserves, substantial growth in Foreign Trade, rationalisation of tariffs, current account convertibility, liberalization of Indian Investments abroad, and enhanced access to external commercial borrowings by Indian corporate and active and significant participation of Foreign Institutional Investors in Indian stock market. The Central Govt. looking at such significant development, decided to bring in Fresh Amendments in the law relating to Foreign Exchange to suit the new environments. The objective was to facilitate the external trade, ease receipts and payments pertaining thereto and promoting orderly and fully organised Foreign Exchange markets.

Thus, the Foreign Exchange Management Act, 1999 (FEMA) which seeks to replace the Foreign Exchange Regulation Act, 1973 (FERA), was brought into effect from 1st June, 2000.

Definitions Pertaining to FEMA

FEMA is an extension to the controversial FERA. It is more liberal & based on the following main definitions.

1. **Authorised Persons:** Any person or any bank or any body which are authorised by RBI to deal in foreign exchange.
2. **Capital Account Transactions:** All those transaction which require forex for purchasing some fixed assets or securities by a person resident in India or outside India. All the capital account transaction is prohibited in FEMA and the permission of RBI is required for all such transactions.
3. **Current Account transactions:**
    - Some of the current account transaction are permitted and do not require permission by RBI. A current account transaction is in connection with foreign trade, current business activities, short term banking and credit facilities in the ordinary course of business, payment of interest on loan, remittances (transfer of money for parents, spouse, children etc.) expenses in connection with foreign travel, education and medical facilities.
    - While some require permission when they cross certain ceiling.
    - Some of the current account transactions are fully prohibited and foreign currency cannot be made available in any case.

4. **Export of goods and services:** The Act requires furnish to RBI the details regarding the exports. Every exporter shall furnish to RBI a declaration containing true and correct material particulars in relation to payment for such services.
5. **Realization and repatriation of foreign Exchange:** Where any amount of foreign exchange is due or approved to any person, he shall takes all reasonable steps to realize or repatriate to India, in time and manner prescribed by Reserve Bank of India.

2.6.1 Power to make regulations

Section 47 of FEMA empowers the Reserve Bank, by notification, to make regulations to carry out the provisions of this Act and the rules there under. Such regulations may provide for

- Permissible classes of capital account transactions, limits of admissibility of foreign exchange for such transactions, and the prohibition, restriction or regulation of certain capital account transactions u/s 6
- Manner and form in which declaration is to be furnished u/s 7 (I)(a)
- period within which and the manner of repatriation of foreign exchange u/s 8
- limit up to which any person may possess foreign currency or foreign coins u/s 9(a)
- Class of persons and limit up to which foreign currency account may be held or operated u/s 9(b)
- limit up to which foreign exchange acquired may be exempted u/s 9(d)
- limit up to which foreign exchange acquired may be retained u/s 9(e)
- Any other matter which is required to be or may be specified.

2.6.2 Salient features of FEMA

- It will facilitate trade rather than prevent misuse of foreign exchange.
- Definitions of capital account transaction and current account transaction have been introduced keeping in mind the possibility of introduction of capital account convertibility in the near future.
- All current account transactions shall be allowed (subject to reasonable restrictions).
- Reserve Bank to classify those capital account transactions that are to be permitted and to regulate transfer and issue of foreign securities by a resident in/outside India as well as setting up of branches/offices by foreign companies in India.
- All key sections relating to dealings, holding and payments in foreign exchange and exports have been simplified.
- Liberalization in enforcement provisions reflects that the attitude is of putting trust in the persons covered

2.7 SECURITIES AND EXCHANGE BOARD OF INDIA

The Securities and Exchange Board of India (SEBI) was established on April 12, 1988 under a resolution of the Government of India. But, it was latter made a statutory body by the Securities and Exchange Board of India Act 1992. According to this Act, the SEBI shall typically consist of a chairman and five other members appointed by the Central Government (Two members representing the ministries of finance and law, one member from the Reserve Bank of India and two other members). With came into effect of the Securities and Exchange Board of India Act 1992, powers and functions exercised by the Central Government with respect of the regulation of the stock exchange operations in India.

2.7.1 Objectives of SEBI

- To protect the interest of Investors.
- To regulate the securities market.
- To promote efficient services by brokers merchant bankers and other Intermediaries.

Management of SEBI

SEBI consist of the chairman and other members (2 members appointed by the govt. representative, 2 the ministry of finance and law, 1 member from RBI and 2 other from Professionals highly qualified in their field of security market).

SEBI act also empowers central govt. to supersede SEBI on account of any policy making, govt. duties etc.

2.7.2 Functions of SEBI

I. Regulatory Functions:

- Regulation of stock exchange and any other security market.
- Registration and regulation of working stock brokers, sub-brokers, registrar to all issue, merchant bankers, under writers, portfolio managers and such other intermediaries who are associated with securities market.
- Registration and regulation of the working of collective investment including mutual funds.
- Prohibition of prudulent and unfair trade practices relating to securities market.
- Prohibit insider trading in securities.
- Regulating substantial acquisitions of shares and takeover of companies.

II. Developmental Functions:

- Promote Investor's education.
- Training of intermediaries.
- Conducting research and its information useful to all market participants.
- Promotion of pair practice and code of conduct for self regulatory organisations.

2.7.3 Powers of SEBI

SEBI vests the following powers:

- Power to call periodical return from recognised stock exchanges.
- Power to call any information or explanation from recognised stock exchanges or their members.
- Power to direct enquiries to be made in relation to affairs of stock exchanges or their member.
- Power to grant approval to byelaws of recognised stock exchanges.
- Power to make or amend byelaws of recognised stock exchanges.
- Power to compel listing of securities of public companies.
- Power to control and regulate stock exchanges.
- Power to grant registration to market intermediaries.
- Power to levy fees or other charges for carrying out the purpose of regulation.
- Power to declare applicability of Section 17 of the Securities Contract (Regulation) Act is any area to grant licences to dealers in securities.

2.8 CONSUMER PROTECTION ACT 1986

The Consumer Protection Act, 1986 was enacted for better protection of the interests of consumers. All the provisions of the Act have come into force from 1 July 1987.

The Act was amended in 1991 and 1993. To make the Consumer Protection Act more functional and purposeful, a comprehensive amendment was carried out in December 2002 and brought into force from 15 March 2003. As a sequel, the Consumer Protection Rules, 1987 were also amended and notified on 5 March 2004.

2.8.1 Rights of Consumers

1. Right to be protected against the marketing of goods and services which are hazardous to life and property
2. Right to be informed about the quality, quantity, potency, purity, standard and price of goods or services so as to protect the consumers against unfair trade practices.
3. Right to be assured, wherever possible, access to a variety of good and services at competitive prices.
4. Right to be heard and to be assured that consumers' interests will receive due consideration at the appropriate forum.
5. Right to seek redressal against unfair trade practices or unscrupulous exploitation of consumers.
6. Right to consumer education.

2.8.2 Salient Feature of Consumer Protection Act 1986

1. It applies to all goods and services unless specifically exempted by the Central Government.
2. It covers all the sectors whether private, public, and cooperative or any person. The provisions of the Act are compensatory as well as preventive and punitive in nature.
3. The Act also envisages establishment of Consumer Protection Councils at the central, state and district levels, whose main objectives will be to promote and protect the rights of consumers.
4. To provide a simple, speedy and inexpensive redressal of consumer grievances, the Act envisages three-tier quasi-judicial machinery at the national, state and district levels. These are: National Consumer Disputes Redressal Commission known as National Commission, State Consumer Disputes Redressal Commissions known as State Commissions and District Consumer Disputes Redressal Forum known as District Forum.
5. The provisions of this Act are in addition to and not in derogation of the provisions of any other law for the time being in force.

UNIT-3

Planning in India

3.1 INTRODUCTION

The philosophy behind economic planning recognizes that markets and price system alone cannot ensure welfare of the citizens of a state. While individuals are the best judges of what is good for them, the sum total of such judgement need not be the best option for the society as a whole. Moreover, areas like infrastructure require large investments without immediate tangible returns and therefore do not attract private investment. This requires the state to step in either directly as in the past or through private-public partnership, which is the principle behind the build operate-transfer (BOT) type of infrastructure development. Finally, the government provides for some goods called public goods, such as the quality of environment and national defences which can be enjoyed by one person without depriving others of similar enjoyment.

The credit for concretising ideas on national planning goes to **Sri M.Visvesvaraya** the visionary engineer and statesman of Mysore who published his Planned Economy for India in 1934, which was a blue-print for a ten-year programme of planned economic development for India.

Indian National Congress set up a National Planning Commission as far back as 1938 with Jawaharlal Nehru Chairman. Over the next decade, there were several initiatives. The most important were:

- 'A Plan for Economic Development in India (1944), popularly known as **the Bombay Plan** which gave priority to the development of basic industries, while at the same time seeking the doubling of agricultural production and of per capita income within a 15 years' framework.
- **The People's Plan** drafted by **Shri M N Roy** which had a 10-year period and which sought to give greatest priority to agriculture. It advocated the nationalization of all agricultural production and distribution.

- **The Gandhian Plan** drafted by Sriman Narayan emphasized economic decentralization with primacy to rural development through the development of cottage industries

3.1.1 Types of Planning

Some of the important types of planning (not mutually exclusive) are described below:

- **Imperative planning** involves centralized planning and implementation as opposed to indicative planning which only lays down the broad goals, strategies and guidelines for achieving the goals.
- **Fixed term plans** are drawn up for a particular period (five years in India) whereas a rolling plan will be more flexible in its targets and allow extension of implementation period.
- **Structural planning** refers to a strategy, which involves the need to change existing institutions or creating new ones. On the other hand, functional planning seeks to achieve the objectives within the existing institutional framework (i.e., without changing existing laws, for instance).
- **Apex planning** or centralized planning envisages only a central institution while multilevel planning allows for decentralized planning. The Panchayati Raj institutions seek to strengthen multi-level planning.

3.1.2 A Review of Five Year Plans

3.1.2.1 First Plan (1951-56)

- Highest priority to agriculture, irrigation and power projects.
- 44.6% of total public sector outlay of Rs. 2069 crores (subsequently increased to Rs. 2378 crores) on agriculture, irrigation and power.
- Transport and communication received 26.4% and industry only 2.8%
- Rate of investment targeted at 7% of national income.
- National income grew by 18% and per capita income by 11%
- Food production went up by 20%

3.1.2.2 Second Plan (1956-61)

- Targeted a 25% increase in national income through rapid industrialization. Actual achievement was only 20%
- Adopted the socialistic pattern of society as the goal.
- Rate of investment planned to be raised from seven percent to 11% of national income.
- National Income increased by almost 20% but per capita income rose only by eight percent.
- Large industries including steel plants (Durgapur, Bhilai and Rourketa) were set up. The locomotive factory at Chittaranjan and Coach Factory at Perambur were other major projects of this period.

3.1.2.3 Third Plan (1961-66)

- Emphasis on basic industries continued but agriculture and allied sectors (irrigation and power) were allocated 35% of the outlay.
- A series of crises – China war (1962) Nehru's death (196) – marred the smooth implementation of the plan.
- Growth rate of only 2.2% achieved as against a target of 5% per annum.
- Inflation (36%) ate up much of the achievement; Rupee devaluation (1966) Annual Plans (1966-69) after the disastrous experience of the Third Plan, a plan holiday was declared for three years. All available resources were mobilized for building a buffer stock and for stepping up food production learning from the experience of near-famine years (1965-66).

Favourable monsoon and technological break-through in wheat popularly known as 'green revolution' reduced the inflationary pressure. Nationalisation of banks was another major step during this period.

3.1.2.4 Fourth Plan (1969-74)

- Emphasis on growth with distributive justice.
- Substantial increases in the outlay for family planning (Rs. 278 crores from Rs. 25 crores in third plan).
- Poor achievement of targets – national income grew by 3.3% per annum; per capital income by 1.2% per annum; agricultural production by 2.8%; industrial production by 3.9%.

3.1.2.5 Fifth Plan (1974-79)

- Twin objectives of poverty eradication and attainment of self-reliance.
- A National Programme for Minimum Needs including elementary education, safe drinking water health care, shelter for landless, and slum up graduation.
- A growth rate of 5.2% (against a target of 4.4%) achieved.
- Agricultural production increased by 4.2% - the highest so far.
- Moderate inflation of 2.1% per annum during the Emergency years (1975-1977)
- The Janata Government terminated the Plan in 1978.

3.1.2.6 Sixth Plan (1980-85)

- Janata Government had adopted a Sixth Plan (1978-83), which was conceived as rolling plan. Mrs. Gandhi's Government in 1980 abandoned this and a new sixth plan was drafted.
- Poverty alleviation given the top priority.
- Schemes for transferring skills (TRYSEM) and assets (IRDP) and providing slack season employment (NREP).
- Actual growth of national income was higher at 5.3% (against a target of 5.2%)

- Increase of 16% per annum in real investment in fixed asset by private sector.
- Poverty declined from 48.3% in 1977-78 to 37.4% in 1983-84.

3.1.2.7 Seventh Plan (1985-90)

- Strong emphasis on creation of productive employment on farm as well as rural subsidiary occupations.
- Stress on increasing the production of food grains, oilseeds, sugar, textiles, domestic fuel and housing.
- Outward-looking strategy with exports receiving high priority.
- Tempo of domestic and external liberalization has tended.
- The plan also had a 15-year perspective (1985-2000) for removal of poverty, providing for basic needs, achieving universal elementary education and total access to health facilities.
- Average annual growth rate during the plan period was 5.6% (target fiver percent)
- Agriculture grew at 4.1% against a target of four percent.
- Manufacturing industries achieved a growth rate of 8.8% (target 8%)
- There was a severe short fall in the mining sector (5.6% against a target of 13%).
- Social sector performance fell far short of targets especially in housing for the landless elementary education, and general poverty alleviation.

3.1.2.8 Eighth Plan (1992-97)

The plan was launched in 1992 after the plan holiday during economically and politically difficult days of 1990-91 and 91-92.

The acceptance of liberation and the need for market forces to play a greater role.

- Employment generation to be speeded up to achieve full employment by 2000.
- Total literacy to be achieved in the 15-35 age groups by covering an additional 110 million people.
- Restructuring the systems of economic management through public sector reforms, including selective disinvestment.
- The English Plan was to walk on 'two legs' – one leg of alleviating poverty and removing unemployment and the other 'leg' providing a 'safety net' for those who will be affected by the structural adjustment programme. The plan had thus built in 'the human face' element of adjustment.

3.1.2.9 Ninth Plan (1997-2002)

- The development strategy emphasized the role for markets and the need for government to intervene to promote a degree of competition through suitable legislation. Licence Raj was to be ended. The plan emphasized co-operative federalism. It also stressed the importance of infrastructural development.

- The plan was indicative in nature, focusing on policies. It also provided a 15-year perspective. It aimed to achieve a growth rate of eight percent per annum in the medium term and a rate of 6.5percent during the plan period ('97-02')

3.1.2.10 Tenth Plan (2002-07)

- Annual 8.1 percent GDP growth during 2002-07.
- Annual FDI flows of 7.5 billion US dollars.
- Public sector outlay at Rs. 15,92,300 crore.
- States and UT outlay at Rs. 6,71,009 crore.
- Literacy rate to increase to 75 percent by 2007.
- Maternal mortality Rate to be reduced to 45 in 2007 and 25 by 2012.
- Reduction in gender gaps in literacy ad wage rates by at least 50 percent by 2007.
- Cleaning of major polluted river stretches.
- Reduction in Government dis-savings to -0.5 percent.
- Increase in tax-GDP ratio to 10.3 percent by 2007.

3.1.3 Features of Tenth Plan

The Tenth Plan has a number of new features:

- Firstly, the Plan recognises the rapid growth in the labour force over the next decade.
- The Tenth Plan, therefore, aims at creating 50 million job opportunities during the period, by placing special emphasis on employment intensive sectors of agriculture, irrigation, agro-forestry, small and medium enterprises, information and communication technology and other services.
- Secondly, the Plan addresses the issue of poverty and the unacceptably low levels of social indicators.
- Thirdly, Tenth Plan has adopted a differential development strategy. It is also for the first time that state wise growth and other monitor able targets have been worked out in consultation with the States.
- This Plan is the recognition that Governance is perhaps one of the most important factors for ensuring that the Plan is realised. The Plan has laid down a perspective list of reforms in this connection.
- Finally, considering the present market-oriented economy, the Tenth Plan has dwelt at length about the policies that would be necessary and the design of key institutions.
- The Tenth Plan not only includes a carefully crafted medium term macroeconomic policy stance, both for the Centre and the States, but also lays out the policy and institutional reforms that are required for each sector.

3.1.4 Approach Paper to 11th Plan

Planning Commission recently approved the approach paper to the Eleventh Five Year Plan beginning in 2007-08. It has clearly set an ambitious target of achieving ten per cent economic growth by the last year of the plan-that is 2011-12. Prime Minister Manmohan Singh, who chairs the full planning commission, said that two areas that require immediate attention were Agriculture and infrastructure. The industry and services sectors in the country are doing well clocking double-digit growth.

1. **Agriculture sector:** It is the agriculture sector, which needs a thrust as the growth rate has virtually stagnated in the sector. If the GDP growth is to be pushed up by 1-2 per cent, it is the agriculture, which has to grow by at least 4 per cent annually on a sustained basis.
   - As over 60 per cent of the population is still dependent on agriculture, it is important that rural India grows rapidly to ensure growth is all inclusive and that gap between rural and urban areas, rich and poor are narrowed down.
   - There has been emphasis on the need for vocational education and skill development to ensure greater employment.
   - The current agrarian crisis can be tackled only if the centrality of state intervention was recognized howsoever inefficient may be.
   - Food security and stability of essential commodity prices are equally important and the approach paper seems to have adopted kid-glove approach in dealing with the issue.
   - The country would have to move towards single common market for farm produce.
   - There is also the need to encourage food processing industries and a separate action plan is needed to boost this sector. Nearly 35-40% of fruits and vegetables produced in the country go as waste.
2. **Employment Generation:** It proposes to create 70 million new work opportunities.
3. **Infrastructure:** It proposes to provide electricity connections to all villages and below poverty line household by 2009 and round the clock power by the end of the plan and telephone connectivity to every village by November 2007 and broadband connectivity to all villages by 2012.
4. **Fiscal Sector:** The approach paper estimates that the gross budgetary support for the Plan (Centre and states combined) would have to increase by 2.5 percentage points of GDP above the Tenth Plan period.
5. **The issue of Fiscal Prudence:** The Approach paper has also recognized the difficulties posed by the rigid FRBM (Fiscal Responsibility and Budget Management) targets to rein-in on fiscal and revenue deficits. It had even suggested a postponement of the FRBM targets for a period of two years. It has also suggested that the focus on wiping out revenue deficits by 2009 should be abandoned as a number of items of expenditure that contribute to human capital formation are listed as revenue expenditure.

6. **Public Private Partnership:** It is for this reason that the Approach Paper advocated an aggressive effort to promote public private partnership in infrastructure projects due to scarcity of public resources.

3.1.5 Changing Nature of Planning

- In a federal democracy like ours, the principal task of planning is to evolve shared vision among not only the federal units but also among other economic agents, so that the efforts of all the actors become convergent towards the national priorities.
- While the growth process can be made the responsibility of the corporate sector to a greater degree, its direction and distribution are to be steered by planned public intervention, so that regional imbalances are reduced and socio economic inequities are set right. For example, directing the growth of the large industry into the backward areas and technology-intensive areas to realise national goals.
- The nature of instruments available to planners in the implementation has changed. The planning process has to focus on the need for planning for policy, so that the signals that are sent to the economic system induce the various agents to grow in a manner that is consistent with national goals. In particular, investment patterns would be determined by sectoral policies. For example, phasing in rupee convertibility over almost a decade, so that the necessary changes and adjustments can be made.
- Given the federal nature of the Indian context, the role of planning is to develop a common policy stance for the Centre and the States. Alsc, the task of federal policy coordination is central to Indian planning. For example, the need to invite foreign investment in infrastructure areas like power need centre-state coordination as the necessary legislation and administrative changes involve both.
- Lastly, planning at the grass root level, that is participatory, is very crucial for improving the delivery systems and proper use of resources. The role of the Government is thus to facilitate participatory planning.

With the change in the role of the State, the function of planning for the development of the country also is undergoing change, particularly since the commencement of the economic reforms in 1991 in India. There has been a national debate about the 'relevance of planning' in the changing context of economic liberalization.

3.2 INDUSTRIAL POLICY

Industrial policy is an important document which lays a wide canvas and set the tone for implementing promotional and regulatory role of the government.

The term industrial policy refers to the to the government policy towards industry-their establishment functioning, growth and management. The policy will indicate the respective areas of large, medium and small scale sector. It will also spell out government policy towards foreign capital, labour, tariff and other related aspects. Naturally the industrial development of a country will be shaped, guided, fostered, regulated and controlled by its industrial policy.

3.2.1 Rational for the industrial policy

1. Direct the flow of scare resources in the most desirable areas of investment in accordance with national priorities.
2. Prevent the wasteful use of scare resources and ensured their conservation and judicious utilisation.
3. Demarcate areas among the public, private and joint sector of the economy, as well as large, medium and small scale industries.
4. Prevent through fiscal and monitory policy, the formation of monopoly and concentration of wealth in a few hand shows that the evils associated with monopolies can be effectively curbed.
5. Empower the government to regulate the establishment and expansion of private industry in accordance to the plant objectives.
6. Correct the imbalances in the development of industries and help bring about a desirable balance and diversification in them.

3.2.2 Industrial Policy Resolution of 1948

After independence the first industrial policy was declared on 6th April 1948 by then union industry minister Mr. Shyama Prasad mukherjee. This policy clearly divided the industrial policy in to private and public sector. This policy established mixed and control economy in the country. The main feature of the industrial policy 1948 is given under the following-

1. Acceptance of the importance of the both private and public sectors
2. Division of the industrial sector
3. Role of small cottage industries
4. Other important features of industrial policy

1. **Acceptance of the important of both private and public sector:** country realised at that time that public and private both are important for the industrial development and they have nearly equal contribution in the development of the country. Their importance cannot be neglected from any angle because they have their own importance in their own field. There are many such as sectors where public sector is not running good but private sector is running very well. Like in banking sectors. At was the very early time of their freedom so the economic condition of the country was very poor. So it was needed to improve the industrial sector in order to improve economy.
2. **Division of the industrial sector:** Industrial policy divided the industrial sector into four major factors.
   I. **Industries where central had monopoly:** in this category three fields of activity were specified arms and ammunition atomic energy and rail transport. Government have decided that the manufacture of arms and ammunition, the production and control of atomic energy, and ownership and management of railway

transport should be the exclusive monopoly of the Central Government. Further in any emergency, the Government would always have the power to take over any industry vital for national defence.

II. **Mixed sector:** In this category six industries were specified.

1. Coal (the India Coalfields Committee's proposals will be generally followed).
2. Iron and Steel.
3. Aircraft manufacture
4. Shipbuilding.
5. Manufacture of telephone, telegraph and wireless apparatus, excluding radio receiving sets.
6. Mineral oils.

While the inherent right of the State to acquire any existing industrial undertaking will always remain, and will be exercised whenever the public interest requires it, Government have decided to let existing undertakings in these fields develop for a period of ten years, during which they will be allowed all facilities for efficient working and reasonable expansion. At the end of this period, the whole matter will be reviewed and a decision taken in the light of circumstances obtaining at the time. If it is decided that the State should acquire any unit, the fundamental rights guarantee by the Constitution will be observed and compensation will be awarded on a fair and equitable basis.

Management of State enterprise will, as a rule, be through the medium of public corporations under the statutory control of the Central Government, who will assume such powers as may be necessary to ensure this.

III. **The field of the government control:** There are certain basic industries of importance, the planning and regulation of which by the Central Government is necessary in the national interest. The following industries whose location must be governed by economic factors of All- India import, or which require considerable investment of a high degree of technical skill, will be the subject of Central regulation and control:

1. Salt
2. Automobiles and tractors
3. Prime movers
4. Electric engineering
5. Other heavy machinery
6. Machine tools
7. Heavy chemicals, fertilizers and pharmaceuticals and drugs
8. Electro-chemical industries
9. Non-ferrous metals
10. Rubber manufactures

11. Power and industrial alcohol
12. Cotton and woollen textiles
13. Cement
14. Sugar
15. Paper and Newsprint
16. Air and Sea transport
17. Minerals
18. Industries related to defence

The above list cannot obviously be of an exhaustive nature. The Government of India, while retaining the ultimate direction over this field of industry, will consult the Governments of the Provinces and States at all stages and fully associate them in the formulations and execution of plant. Besides these Governments, representatives of Industry and Labour will also be associated with the Central bodies which they propose to establish, as recommended by the Industries Conference.

3.2.3 Industrial Policy Resolution of 1956

Later on 1948 industrial policy was replaced by a new industrial policy Resolution declared on April 30, 1956 with the basic objective of establishing "Socialistic Pattern of Society" in the country. Industrial policy resolution of 1956 categorised industries which would be the exclusive responsibility of the state or would progressively come under state control. The preeminent position of the public sector it envisaged private sector co exiting with the state and thus attempted to give flexibility to the policy framework. Though the government had Eight years have passed since this deflation on industrial policy. These eight years have witnessed many important changes and developments in India. The constitution of India has been enacted, guaranteeing certain fundamental rights and enunciating Directive Principles of State Policy. Planning has proceeded on an organised basis, and the first Five Year Plan has recently been completed. Parliament has accepted the socialist pattern of society as the objective of social and economic policy. These important developments necessitate a fresh statement of industrial policy, more particularly as the Second Five Year Plan will soon be placed before the country. This policy must be governed by the principles laid down in the Constitution, the objective of socialism and the experience gained during these years.

The Constitution of India, in its preamble, has declared that it aims at securing for all its citizens:

"**JUSTICE**, social, economic and political;
"**LIBERTY**, of thoughts, expression, belief, faith and worship;
"**EQUALITY,** of status and of opportunity and to promote among them all;
"**FRATERNITY**, assuring the dignity of the individual and the unity of the Nation;

In its Directive Principles of State Policy, it is stated that–

"The State shall strive to promote the welfare of the people by securing and protecting as effectively as it may a social order in which justice, social, economic and political, shall inform all the institutions of the national life."

Further That

"The State shall, in particular, direct its policy towards securing:

1. that the citizens, men and women equally, have the right to an adequate means of livelihood;
2. That the ownership and control of the material resources of the community are so distributed as best to sub serve the common good:
3. that the operation of the economic system does not result in the concentration of wealth and means of production to the common detriment;
4. That there is equal pay for equal work for both men women;
5. That the health and strength of workers, men and women, and the tender age of children are not abused and that citizens are not forced by economic necessity to enter vocations unsuited to their age of strength:
6. That childhood and youth are protected against exploitation and against moral and material abandonment."

Categorization of industries

In the 1956 policy, industries were classified into three categories

1. Schedule A
2. Schedule B
3. Private sector unit

Schedule A

Industries in the first category have been listed in Schedule A of this Resolution. All new units in these industries, save where their establishment in the private sector has already been approved, will be set up only by the State. This does not preclude the expansion of the existing privately owned units, or the possibility of the State securing the co-operation of private enterprise in the establishment of new units when the national interests so require. Railways and air transport, arms and ammunition and atomic energy will, however, be developed as Central Government monopolies. Whenever cooperation with private enterprise is necessary, the State will ensure, either through majority participation in the capital or otherwise, that it has the requisite powers to guide the policy and control the operations of the undertakings.

These are the 17 industries which are categorised in schedule A.

1. Arms and ammunition and allied items of defence equipments.
2. Atomic energy.

3. Iron and Steel.
4. Heavy castings and forgings of iron and steel.
5. Heavy plant and machinery required for iron and steel production, for mining, for machinery tool manufacture and for such other basic industries as may be specified by the Central Government.
6. Heavy electrical plant including large hydraulic and steam turbines.
7. Coal and lignite.
8. Mineral oils.
9. Mining of iron ore, manganese ore, crome-ore, gypsum, sulphur, gold and diamond.
10. Mining and processing of copper, lead, zinc, tin, molybdenum and wolfram.
11. Minerals specified in the Schedule to the Atomic Energy (Control of production and Use) Order, 1953.
12. Aircraft.
13. Air transport.
14. Railway transport.
15. Shipbuilding.
16. Telephones and telephones cables telegraph and wireless apparatus (excluding radio receiving sets).
17. Generation and distribution of electricity.

Schedule B

In this category these industries are mentioned. Industries in the second category will be those listed in Schedule B. With a view to accelerating their future development, the State will increasingly establish new undertakings in these industries. At the same time, private enterprise will also have the opportunity to develop in this field, either on its own or with State participation.

1. All other minerals except 'minor minerals' as defined in Section 3 of the Minerals Concession Rules 1949.
2. Aluminium and other non-ferrous metals not included in Schedule A.
3. Machine tools.
4. Ferro-alloys and tool steels.
5. Basic and intermediate products required by chemical industries such as the manufacture of drugs, dye-stuffs and plastics.
6. Antibiotics and other essential drugs.
7. Fertilizers
8. Synthetic rubber.
9. Carbonization of coal.
10. Road transport

11. Chemical pulp.
12. Sea transport.

Private sector

In this sector those industries were kept which are not included in schedule

A. and schedule

B. but this sector is open for both private and government.

3.2.4 Industrial Policy Resolution of February 2, 1973

1. The Industrial Policy Resolution of 1956 still remained valid, but certain structural distortions had crept in the system.
2. The new policies were hence directed towards removing these distortions.
3. It provided for a closer interaction between the agricultural and industrial sectors.
4. Accorded the highest priority to the generation and transmission of power.
5. An exhaustive analysis of industrial products was made to identify products which are capable of being produced in the small scale sector.
6. The list of industries exclusively reserved for the small scale sector was expanded from 180 items to more than 500 items.
7. Within the small scale sector, a tiny sector was also defined with investment in machinery and equipment up to Rs.1 lakh and situated in towns with a population of less than 50,000 according to 1971 census figures, and in villages.
8. Special legislation to protect cottage and household industries was also proposed to be introduced.
9. It was also decided that compulsory export obligations, merely for ensuring the foreign exchange balance of the project, would no longer be insisted upon while approving new industrial capacity.
10. In the areas of price control of agricultural and industrial products, the prices would be regulated to ensure an adequate return to the investor.

3.2.5 Industrial Policy Resolution of December 23, 1977

1. Industrial Policy Highlights on producing inputs needed by a large number of smaller units and making adequate marketing arrangements.
2. The nucleus plant would also work for upgrading the technology of small units.
3. The Government would promote the development of a system of linkages between nucleus large plants and the satellite ancillaries.
4. To boost the development of small scale industries, the investment limit in the case of tiny units was enhanced to Rs.2 lakh, of small scale units to Rs.20 lakh and of ancillaries to Rs.25 lakh.

5. A scheme for building buffer stocks of essential raw materials for the Small Scale Industries was introduced for operation through the Small Industries Development Corporations in the States and the National Small Industries Corporation in the Centre.
6. Industrial processes and technologies aimed at optimum utilisation of energy or the exploitation of alternative sources of energy would be given special assistance, including finance on concessional terms.

3.2.6 Industrial Policy Resolution of July 1980

It was based on the Industrial Policy Resolution of 1956

1. Optimum utilisation of installed capacity;
2. Maximum production and achieving higher productivity;
3. Higher employment generation;
4. Correction of regional imbalances;
5. Strengthening of the agricultural base through agro based industries and promotion of optimum inter-sect oral relationship;
6. Promotion of export-oriented industries;
7. Promotion of economic federalism through equitable spread of investment and dispersal of returns
8. Consumer protection against high prices and bad quality.

3.2.7 Industrial Policy Resolution of 1991

Policy Objectives

1. In 1984, immediately after Independence, Government introduced the Industrial Policy Resolution. This outlined the approach to industrial growth and development. It emphasised the importance to the economy of securing a continuous increase in production and ensuring its equitable distribution. After the adoption of the Constitution increase in production and ensuring its equitable distribution. After the adoption of the Constitution and the socioeconomic goals, the Industrial Policy was comprehensively revised and adopted in 1956. To meet new challenges, from time, it was modified through statements in 1973, 1977 and 1980.
2. The Industrial Policy Resolution of 1948 was followed by the Industrial Policy Resolution of 1956 which had as its objective the acceleration of the rate of economic growth and the speeding up of industrialization as a means of achieving a socialist pattern of society. In 1956, capital was scarce and the base of entrepreneurship not strong enough. Hence, the 1956 Industrial policy Resolution gave primacy to the role of the State to assume a predominant and direct responsibility for industrial development.
3. The Industrial Policy Statement of 1973, inter alia, identified high priority industries where investment from large industrial houses and foreign companies would be permitted.

4. The Industrial Policy Statement of 1977 laid emphasis on decentralisation and on the role of small scale, tiny and cottage industries.
5. The Industrial Policy Statement of 1980 focused attention on the need for promoting competition in the domestic market, technological up gradation and modernisation. The policy laid the foundation for an increasingly competitive export base and for encouraging foreign investment in high technology areas. This found expression in the Sixth Five-Year Plan which bore the distinct stamp of Smt. Indira Gandhi. It was Smt. Indira Gandhi who emphasised the need for productivity to be the central concern in all economic and production activities.
6. These policies created a climate for rapid industrial growth in the country. Thus on the eve Of the Seventh Five Year Plan, a board-based infrastructure had been built up. Basic industries had been established. A high degree of self reliance in a large number of items-raw materials, intermediates, and finished goods had been achieved. New growth centres of industrial activity had emerged, as had a new generation of entrepreneurs. A large number of engineers, technicians and skilled workers had also been trained.
7. The Seventh Plan recognised the need to consolidate on these strenths and to take initiatives to prepare Indian industry to respond effectively to the emerging challenges. A number of policy and procedural changes were introduced in 1985 and 1986 under the leadership of Shri Rajiv Gandhi aimed at increasing productivity, reducing costs and improving quality. The accent was on opening the domestic market to increased competition and readying our industry to stand on its own in the face of international competition. The public sector was freed from a number of constraints and given a larger measure of autonomy. The technological and managerial modernisation of industry was pursued as the key instrument for increasing productivity and improving our competitiveness in the world. The net result of all these changes was that Indian industry grew by an impressive average annual growth rate of 8.5% in the Seventh Plan Period.
8. Government is pledged to launching a reinvigorated struggle for social and economic justice, to end poverty and unemployment and to build a modern, democratic, socialist, prosperous and forward-looking India. Such a society can be built if India grows as part of the world economy and not in isolation.
9. While Government will continue to follow the policy of self-reliance, there would be greater emphasis placed on building up our ability to pay for imports through our own foreign exchange earnings. Government is also committed to development and utilisation of indigenous capabilities in technology and manufacturing as well as its up gradation to world standards.
10. Government will continue to pursue a sound policy framework encompassing encouragement of entrepreneurship, development of indigenous technology through investment in research and development, bringing in new technology dismantling of the

regulatory system, development of the capital markets and increasing competitiveness for the benefit of the common man. The spread of industrialisation to backward areas of the country will be actively promoted through appropriate incentives, institutions and infrastructure investments.

11. Government will provide enhanced support to the small-scale sector so that it flourishes in an environment of economic efficiency and continuous technological up gradation.
12. Foreign investment and technology collaboration will be welcomed to obtain higher technology, to increase exports and to expand the production base.
13. Government will endeavour to abolish the monopoly of any sector or any individual enterprise in any field of manufacture, except on strategic or military considerations and open all manufacturing activity to competition.
14. The Government will ensure that the public sector plays its rightful role in the evolving socio-economic scenario of the country. Government will ensure that the public sector is run on business lines as envisaged in the Industrial Policy Resolution of 1956 and would continue to innovate and lead in strategic areas of national importance. In the 1950s and 1960s the principal instrument for controlling the commanding heights of the economy was investment in the capital of key industries. Today, the State has other instruments of intervention, particularly fiscal and monetary instruments. The State also instruments of intervention, particularly fiscal and monetary instruments. The State also commands the bulk of the nation's savings. Banks and financial institutions are under State Control. Where State intervention is necessary, these instruments will prove more effective and decisive.
15. Government will fully protect the interests of labour, enhance their welfare and equip them in all respects to deal with the inevitability of technological change. Government believes that no small section of society can corner the gains of growth, leaving workers to bear its pains. Labour will be made an equal partner in progress and prosperity. Workers participation in management will be promoted. Workers co-operatives will be encouraged to participate in packages designed to turn around sick companies. Intensive training, skill development and up gradation programmes will be launched.
16. Government will continue to visualise new horizons. The major objectives of the new industrial policy package will be to build in the gains already made, correct the distortions or weaknesses that may have crept in, maintain a sustained growth in productivity and gainful employment and attain international competitiveness. The pursuit of these objectives will be tempered by the need to preserve the environment and ensure the efficient use of available resources. All sectors of industry whether small, medium or large, belonging to the public, private or co-operative sector will be encouraged to grow and improve on their past performance.
17. Government's policy will be continuity with change.

18. In pursuit of the above objectives, Government have decided to take a series of initiatives in respect of the policies relating to the following areas.
    1. Industrial Licensing.
    2. Foreign Investment.
    3. Foreign Technology Agreements.
    4. Public Sector Policy.
    5. MRTP Act.

3.3 SMALL-SCALE INDUSTRY

The definition for small-scale industrial undertakings has changed over time. Initially they were classified into two categories- those using power with less than 50 employees and those not using power with the employee strength being more than 50 but less than 100. However, the capital resources invested on plant and machinery buildings have been the primary criteria to differentiate the small-scale industries from the large and medium scale industries.

An industrial unit can be categorized as a small- scale unit if it fulfils the capital investment limit fixed by the Government of India for the small-scale sector.

As per the latest definition which is effective since December 21, 1999, for any industrial unit to be regarded as Small Scale Industrial unit the following condition is to be satisfied: -

Investment in fixed assets like plants and equipments either held on ownership terms on lease or on hire purchase should not be more than Rs 10 million.

However the unit in no way can be owned or controlled of any other industrial unit.

Year Investment Limits

1960	Upto Rs 5 lacs in	Plant & Machinery
1966	Upto Rs 7.5 lacs in	Plant & Machinery
1975	Upto Rs 10 lacs in	Plant & Machinery
1980	Upto Rs 20 lacs in	Plant & Machinery
1985	Upto Rs 35 lacs in	Plant & Machinery
1991	Upto Rs 60 lacs in	Plant & Machinery
1997	Upto Rs 100 lacs in	Plant & Machinery
1999	Upto Rs 100 lacs in	Plant & Machinery

Importance of SSI

- These industries have huge employment potential.
- The capital output ratio is considerably high.
- These industries ensure maximum utilization of locally available resources.
- These industries can the developed in almost all the areas including backward, tribal, and hilly areas.

- There by reducing regional imbalances.
- They create less ecological problems.
- They increase the pace of rural development.

3.3.1 Measures of Small-Scale Units

1. **Reservation of Products:** Protection has been provided to the small-scale units by the reservation of items for exclusive production in small scale sector. Over the gears there had been an increase in number of items so reserved, but has significantly reduced it recently.
2. **Machinery on Hire Purchase:** The National small Industries Corporation (NSIC) arrange supply of machines on hire purchase to small scale units.
3. **Marketing Assistance:** Including export promotion assistance are provided by institutions. Such as NSIC Small Industries Development organization (SIDO), kvic etc.
4. **Supply of Raw Materials:** Arrangements have also been made for the supply of raw materials, particularly of scarce items, to the small scale units.
5. **Training:** Training for existing & potential entrepreneurs and others associated with the working of small units are offered by Entrepreneurship Development Institute of India (EDII), Technical Consultancy Organisations (TCOs), financial institutions and commercial banks, etc.

3.3.2 Role of Small-Scale Industries in Indian Economy

The small-scale industrial sector plays a pivotal role in the Indian economy in terms of employment and growth has recorded a high rate of growth since Independence in spite of stiff competition from large-scale industries. There are several important reasons why these industries are contributing a lot to the progress of the Indian economy:

1. **Production:** The small-scale industries sector plays a vital role in the growth of the country. It contributes almost 40% of the gross industrial value added in the Indian economy. It has been estimated that a million Rs. of investment in fixed assets in the small scale sector produces 4.62 million worth of goods or services with an approximate value addition of ten percentage points.

   The small-scale sector has grown rapidly over the years. The growth rates during the various plan periods have been very impressive. The number of small-scale units has increased from an estimated 0.87 million units in the year 1980-81 to over 3 million in the year 2000.
2. **Employment:** SSI Sector in India creates largest employment opportunities for the Indian populace, next only to Agriculture. It has been estimated that 100,000 rupees of investment in fixed assets in the small-scale sector generates employment for four persons.
3. **Export:** SSI Sector plays a major role in India's present export performance. SSI Sector contributes 45%-50% of the Indian Exports. Direct exports from the SSI Sector account for nearly 35% of total exports. Besides direct exports, it is estimated that small-scale industrial

units contribute around 15% to exports indirectly. This takes place through merchant exporters, trading houses and export houses. They may also be in the form of export orders from large units or the production of parts and components for use for finished exportable goods.

4. **Opportunity:** The opportunities in the small-scale sector are enormous due to the following factors:
   - Less Capital Intensive
   - Extensive Promotion & Support by Government
   - Reservation for Exclusive Manufacture by small scale sector
   - Project Profiles
   - Funding - Finance & Subsidies
   - Machinery Procurement
   - Raw Material Procurement
   - Manpower Training
   - Technical & Managerial skills
   - Tooling & Testing support
   - Reservation for Exclusive Purchase by Government
   - Export Promotion

3.3.3 Problems of SSI

Small enterprises are presently seriously handicapped in comparison with larger units by an inequitable allocation system for scarce raw materials and imported components, lack of provision of credit and finance; low technical skill and managerial ability; and marketing contracts. It is, therefore, essential to develop an overall approach to remove these disabilities.

1. **Output vs Employment:** One argument is that the emphasis on employment is irrelevant, as the basic thing is the output that the economy needs for its growth. From this angle, it is contended that, since the productivity of these industries is low compared to that of large industries, the small industries simply waste the capital which is very scarce, and which, if diverted to large industries, can produce more. From this viewpoint, small industries are more capital-intensive. It is also argued that the labour-productivity in the small industries is also small compared to large industries.

2. **Adverse effect on Capital:** It is also contended by some that small industries have unfavourable consequences on saving and capital formation. They argue that the establishment of these industries will, over a period of time, reduce the availability of capital for large-scale industries with higher productivity of capital.

   First, it will happen because capital, used inefficiently in the small industries, will not be available for large-scale industries. *Second,* these industries being labour-intensive, use a major proportion of the sale proceeds of output to pay workers whose marginal propensity to save is low. As a result, a large part of their incomes will be used for consumption resulting in a lower rate of saving and capital formation for the economy.

3. **Inefficient Production:** Another charge against these industries is that the cost of production is higher than in the large industries, because these industries suffer from several inefficiencies. No doubt, the fact of large scale entails, what is described as economies of scale, lowering the costs.
4. **Large Sickness:** There are two main issues in respect of sick SSIs: (i) existence of a large number of sick units which are non-viable; and (ii) rehabilitation of potentially viable units. As far as former is concerned, there were 1, 67,980 sick SSI units as on March 31, 2003. These units are those that had obtained loans from banks. An amount of Rs. 5,706 crore was blocked in these units. Of these, as many as 1,62,791 units with outstanding bank credit of Rs. 4,569 crore were identified by banks as being non-viable. As far as the latter issue is concerned, of the 1,67,980 sick SSI units as on March 31, 2003, only 3,626 units with outstanding bank credit of Rs. 625 crore were found to be potentially viable by the banks.
5. **Several Difficulties:** It is thus obvious that these industries, despite their importance in the economy, are not contributing to their full towards the development of the country along the desirable lines. It is because these are beset with a number of problems concerning their operations. These may be described as under:
   - **Inadequacy of finance**
   - **Difficulties of Marketing**
   - **Shortage of raw materials**
   - **Low-level technology**
   - **Competition from large-scale industries**

3.4 MONETARY POLICY

The strategys of influencing movsements of the money supply and interest rates to affect output and inflation. Aim of this policy is to smooth the supply of credits to the business to boosts Trade & Industry in India.

- The part of the economic policy which regulates the level of money in the economy in order to regulate inflation, improve balance of payments, increase gross national product etc.
- RBI reserves its right to alter monetary policy to time to time depending upon state of economy.

"Def Harry G. Johnson: Policy employing the central banks control of the supply of money as an instrument for achieving the objective of general economic policy"

3.4.1 Type of Monetary Policy

1. **Tight Monetary Policy:** Is also called concretionary monetary policy, tends to curb inflation by contracting the money supply.
2. **Easy Monetary Policy:** Is also called expansionary monetary policy, tends to encourage growth by expanding the money supply.

3.4.1 Objectives of Monetary Policy

There are some monetary policies in developing countries they are:

1. **Price stability:** Inflation distorts economic calculation and expectations while deflation creates depression in the economy. So both inflation and deflation are harmful for the economy. Thus, price stability should be main aim of monetary policy. Prices stability promotes business confidence, makes economic calculations possible, control business cycle and introduces certainty in the economic life.
2. **Exchange stability:** Maintenance of stable exchange rates is an essential condition for the creation of international confidence and promotion of smooth international trade on the largest scale possible.
3. **Full employment:** In under develop countries like Bangladesh the full employment objective is more crucial, because such economies have both un-employment and under-employment open and disguised. In less develop countries though full employment cannot be achieved within a short period, the monetary policy should try to achieve at least a near full employment situation.
4. **Economic growth:** This is comparatively a recent objective of monetary policy. It refers to the growth of real income or output per capita. Monetary policy can contribute to economic growth in a efficient way.
5. **Neutrality of money:** Neutrality of money indicates a situation in which changes in the quantity of money in such a way as to cause a proportionate change in the equilibrium prices of commodities and the equilibrium rate of interest remain unchanged. If money is neutral, an increase or decrease in the quantity of money will not produce any disturbing effect in the economy.

5. **Balance of payment equilibrium:** Balance of payment equilibrium condition is a position at which a country repaid its debt and has attained an adequate reserve at zero balance over time. This objective on monetary policy has become significance in the post war period.

3.4.3 Effectiveness of Monetary Policy

The experience of under developed and developing countries reveals that a credit policy framed by RBI suffers from following lacunas:

- Large non-magnetized sectors serve as a tool of failure for monetary policy in several sectors.

- Underdeveloped money and capital markets, which lacks in bills, stocks and shares that, are organized properly.
- Foreign banks: Monetary policy has no control over these foreign banks and large number of public is borrowing from these banks.
- Large number of non-banking financial institution like indigenous bankers is operating in the Indian market and RBI has no control over these people.

3.4.4 Instrument of Monetary Policy

Instrument of monetary policy generally mean the different means of controlling credit in the economy. The instruments are as follows:

1. **Quantitative Instruments:** These instruments influence the credit creating capacity of the commercial banks by affecting directly or indirectly the excess of the banks. Different forms of quantitative instrument are:
   - **Variable reserve ratio:** Banks are legally required to maintain a certain percentage of their deposits in the form of cash. It determines the capacity of banks to make loans or purchase securities. The central bank can influence the credit creation capacity of the commercial banks by controlling the volume of cash reserve and the minimum legal reserve ratio.
   - **Bank rate:** It is the rate at which central bank lends money to the commercial banks. If bank rate is increased it will increases the cost of borrowing of commercial banks, which in turn reduces the capacity of credit creation of the commercial banks. In the opposite way, a reduction in bank rate will increase the amount of credit created by commercial banks.
   - **Open market Operation:** Open market purchase of securities by the central bank will give more power and money in the hands of commercial banks to expand credit creation. The opposite will happen if there are sales of securities by the central bank.
2. **Qualitative Instrument:** It refers to regulation of credit for specific purposes or branches of economic activity. The aim of selective credit control is to discourage such forms of activities, which are considered to be relatively inessential or less desirable.
   - **Lending at low rates to priority sector:** Priority sectors are those sectors which require special attention for the economic development e.g. agriculture, health, education, infrastructure etc are given funds at low interest rates then the commercial lending rates. Govt keeps differential into rate for priority & developed sectors. Priority sectors such as agriculture, health, education, infrastructure, etc. given funds at low into rates then a commercial lending rates. Govt adopts such a policy so that these sectors borrow more for their development purposes.

- **Lending at higher rates to already developed sector:** Govt changes a high rate of interest from the corporate because they have ample amount of money to pay as interest and as well as they invest money in profitable avenues which are well planned.
- **Issue of directives to banks:** RBI issues direction and orders to commercial banks from time to time. If a bank is found indulged in any sort of malpractices then the RBI has the power to issue instruction and prohibit that bank from that activity.
- **Moral suasion:** RBI may prohibit banking companies in entering into certain transactions and generally give advice to any banking company. Moral suasion provides all those methods like letters, periodicals etc to be issued to banks asking them to exercise control over credit for any particular commodities. Discussions are also held with bankers for the same purpose.

3.4.5 Limitations of Monetary Policy

1. **The time lag:** the time taken in checking out the policy action, its implementation and working time. Its divided into two parts:

   I. **Inside tag or preparatory lag:**
   - Identifying nature of probability
   - Identifying sources of probability
   - Choice of appropriate policy action
   - Implementation of policy action

   II. **Outside lag or response lag:** The time taken by households and the firms to react in response to the policy action taken by the monetary authorities. This lag is long.
2. **Problems in forecasting:** Reliable assessment of magnitude of the problem recession or inflation as it helps in determining the appropriate policy measures.
3. **Non-Banking financial intermediaries:** Structural change reduces effectiveness of monetary policy. Although financial intermediaries cannot create credit thro' the process of credit multiplier, their huge share in the financial operations reduces the effectiveness of monetary policy.
4. **Under development of money & capital market:** Effectiveness of monetary policy is less developed countries is reduced considerably because of the under developed character of their money and capital markets.

3.5 FISCAL POLICY

The fiscal policy is wielded by Govt. to maintain health of economy, by ensuring the balance between the supply of money and productive capability of the economy. The term fiscal represents budget, which is the plan of Govt. for expenditure & revenues for a coming year.

"Fiscal policy is the means by which a government adjusts its levels of spending in order to monitor and influence a nation's economy".

"Fiscal policy is that part of government policy which is concerned with razing revenue through taxation and other means and deciding on the level and pattern of expenditure".

"In other wards the term fiscal policy refers to the expenditure a government undertakes to provide goods and services and to the way in which the government finances these expenditures".

3.5.1 Objectives of Fiscal Policy

1. To achieve desirable price level
2. To Achieve desirable consumption level
3. To Achieve desirable employment level
4. To achieve desirable income distribution
5. Increase in capital formation
6. Degree of inflation

3.5.2 Fiscal Policy And Macroeconomic Goals

1. **Economic Growth:** By creating conditions for increase in savings & investment.
2. **Employment:** By encouraging the use of labour absorbing technology.
3. **Stabilization:** fight with depression trends and booming (overheating) indications in the economy.
4. **Economic Equality:** By reducing the income and wealth gaps between the rich and poor.
5. **Price stability:** employed to contain inflationary and deflationary tendencies in the economy.

3.5.3 Instruments of Fiscal Policy

1. **Budget:** Keeping budget in balance, in surplus or deficit, is in itself a fiscal instrument. When the government keeps its total expenditure equal to its revenue, as a matter of policy, it means it has adopted a balanced budget policy. When the government spends more than its expected revenue, as a matter of policy, it is pursuing a deficit-budget policy. And when the government follows a policy of keeping its expenditure substantially below its current revenue, it is following a surplus budget policy.
2. **Taxation:** A tax is a non quid pro quo payment by the people to the government. By this definition, taxation means non quid pro quo transfer of private income to public coffers by means of taxes. Taxation takes many forms in the developed countries including taxation of personal and corporate income, so-called value added taxation and the collection of royalties or taxes on specific sets of goods.

3. **Public Expenditure:** Suppose the government spends more on an electricity project for which the contract is given to a PSU like BHEL. Then the money that the government spends comes back to it in the form of BHEL's earnings. Similarly, suppose that the government spends on food-for-work programmers, and then a significant part of the expenditure allocation would consist of food grain from the Public Distribution System which would account for part of the wages of workers employed in such schemes. This in turn means that the losses of the Food Corporation of India (which also includes the cost of holding stocks) would go down and hence the money would find its way back to the government. In both cases, the increased expenditure has further multiplier effects because of the subsequent spending of those whose incomes go up because of the initial expenditure. The overall rise in economic activity in turn means that the government's tax revenues also increase. Therefore there is no increase in the fiscal deficit in such cases.
4. **Government Borrowing:** Government borrowing is another fiscal Method by which savings of the community may be mobilized for economic development. In developing economies, the government resort to borrowing in order to finances schemes of economic development. Government or what is also called public borrowing becomes necessary because taxation alone cannot provide sufficient funds for economic development. Besides, too heavy taxation has an adverse effect on private saving and investment.

3.5.4 Economic effects of Fiscal Policy

1. Governments use fiscal policy to influence the level of aggregate demand in the economy, in an effort to achieve economic objectives of price stability, full employment, and economic growth.
2. The government can implement these deficit spending policies to stimulate trade due to its size and prestige.
3. In the classical view, fiscal policy also decreases net exports, which has a mitigating effect on national output and income. When government borrowing increases interest rates it attracts foreign capital from foreign investors.

3.6 STOCK EXCHANGE

In India, the only stock exchanges operated in the 19th century were those of Mumbai in 1875 and Ahmedabad setup in 1894. Both stock exchanges were organised as voluntary nonprofit making associations of brokers. The main intention and objectives is to regulate and protect their interests. Bombay Securities Control Act 1925, which was recognised the Bombay Stock Exchange in 1937 and Ahmedabad in 1937. During the war period, a number of stock exchanges were organised even in Mumbai, Ahmedabad and other centers, therefore, they were not recognised. After the Independence the Central Government was passed the Securities Contracts Regulation Act in 1956 in Parliament.

3.6.1 Meaning and Definition of Stock Exchange

A stock exchange is an organisation of brokers and investment bankers which has the purpose of providing the facilities for trade location and record keeping. Trade on exchange is by members only. One is said to "have a seat" on the exchange. In Europe, stock exchanges are often called bourses. The trading of stock on stock exchanges is called the stock market.

Generally, stock exchange is a market in which securities are bought and sold and it is an essential component of a developed capital market.

According to the Securities Contracts (Regulation) Act 1956

Stock exchange means anybody of individuals, whether incorporated or not, constituted for the purpose of assisting, regulating or controlling the business of buying, selling or dealing in securities. According to this Act, securities include the following:

- Shares, scripts, stocks, bonds, debentures, stock or other marketable securities of any incorporated company or corporate
- Government securities
- Right or interest securities

3.6.2 Role and importance of Stock Exchange

- The stock exchange will play an important role in the success of the economy of the country.
- The stock exchange is one of the basic financial tools for stimulating the economy by attracting capital for investment in the projects.
- The stock exchange also helps to revive other sectors of the economy such as commerce, industry and service.
- The stock exchange is attracting foreign capital to the country (India) particularly at present time, when the international companies have shown serious interest in the country as an important place for their investment.
- Shares, scripts, stocks, debentures stock and government securities are traded in stock exchange.
- Stock exchanges are provided appropriate advice to their clients.
- Stock exchange will list public private and foreign companies.
- Stock exchange wish to join the linkage system between the region's stock exchanges and at a later stage, with international stock exchanges.
- Stock exchange is providing a market that mobilises and distributes the nation's savings utilised for the best purpose of the country.
- Stock exchange is a market in which securities are bought and sold.
- The opportunity for stock exchanges to render the services of stimulating private savings and channelizing such savings into productive investment.

3.6.3 Functions of Stock Exchange

- A stock exchange is a very important financial market.
- Stock exchange is a highly efficient and visible instrument of financing.
- Stock exchange is used to finance the most of the needs of corporations, way of above financing available from banks.
- Individuals and firms save some of their income and invest it.
- The stock exchange is a meeting ground for savers wishing to invest their savings-and firms looking for investments.
- Another function of stock exchanges is to assist government in financing their internal borrowing requirements.
- Government sell obligations (called bonds) to investors through the stock exchanges in their countries.
- Stock exchange is an indispensable tool for refinancing national debt.
- Stock exchange is a market in which securities are bought and sold.
- Shares, scripts, stocks, debenture stocks and government securities are traded in stock exchange.

3.6.4 Services of Stock Exchange

The stock market occupies a pivotal position in the financial system. It performs several economic functions and renders invaluable services to the investors, companies, and to the economy. The following are the services provided by the stock exchange.

1. **Liquidity and Marketability of Securities:** Stock exchanges provide buying and selling of securities. Stock exchange provides liquidity to securities since securities can be converted into cash at any time according to the discretion of investor by selling them at the listed price. This facility is providing continuous marketability to the investors in respect of securities they hold or intend to hold.
2. **Safety of Funds:** Over trading, illegitimate speculation etc. are prevented through carefully designed set of rules, regulations and the byelaws are meant to ensure safety of investible funds. Therefore, stock exchange is protected investors fund.
3. **Supply of Long Term Funds:** In security market, securities are transferable from one person to another with minimum formalities. When security is sold, one investor is substituted by another. However, the company is assured availability of long term funds.
4. **Flow of Capital to Profitable Venture:** The profitability and popularity of companies are reflected in terms of hike in stocks. According to Husband and Dockeray "Stock exchanges function like a traffic signal, indicating a green light when certain fields offer the necessary inducement to attract capital blazing a red light when the outlook for new investments is not attractive."
5. **Motivation for Improved Performance:** The performance of a company is reflected in terms of prices quoted in the stock market. Stock exchange always encourages

improving performance of companies. Because public can expect to invest in growth companies.

6. **Promotion of Investment:** Stock exchanges mobilise the savings from the public into effective production purpose. In this way, stock exchange can promote investment through capital formation.
7. **Reflection of Business Cycle:** The changing economic and business conditions are immediately reflected on the stock exchanges. Stock exchange identifies the booms and depressions of the economy. The government can take suitable monetary and fiscal policies which can help to investors.
8. **Marketing of New Issues:** If the new issues are listed in stock exchange. Stock exchanges ready to accept and their evaluation by concerned stock exchange authorities. Stock market always helps in marketing of new issues.

   I. **Miscellaneous Issues:** Stock exchange encourages public to mobilise their savings. It guides investors in choosing securities by supplying the daily quotation of list of securities. It exhibits recent trends of the companies in the business.

3.6.5 Organisation Structure of Stock Exchange

The organisation structure of stock exchanges is different from place to place. Different forms are:

- **Voluntary non-profit making association:** 3 Stock Exchanges.
- **Public Limited Company:** 14 Stock Exchanges.
- **Company Limited by Guarantee:** 6 Stock Exchanges Mumbai, Ahmedabad and Indore are three recognised Stock Exchanges. These are the voluntary non-profit making associations. Calcutta, Delhi, Bangalore, Cochin, Kanpur, Ludhiana, Guwahati Stock Exchanges are the examples of Public Limited Company/Joint Stock Companies Limited by Shares. Hyderabad, Mumbai and Pune Stock Exchanges are the examples of the Companies Limited by Guarantee.

3.7 BOMBAY STOCK EXCHANGE

The Bombay Stock Exchange is known as the oldest exchange in Asia. It traces its history to the 1850s, when stockbrokers would gather under banyan trees in front of Mumbai's Town Hall. The location of these meetings changed many times, as the number of brokers constantly increased. The group eventually moved to Dalal Street in 1874 and in 1875 became an official organization known as 'The Native Share & Stock Brokers Association'. In 1956, the BSE became the first stock exchange to be recognized by the Indian Government under the Securities Contracts Regulation Act.

The Bombay Stock Exchange developed the BSE Sensex in 1986, giving the BSE a means to measure overall performance of the exchange. In 2000 the BSE used this index to open its derivatives market, trading Sensex futures contracts. The development of Sensex options along with equity derivatives followed in 2001 and 2002, expanding the BSE's trading platform. Historically an open-cry floor trading exchange, the Bombay Stock Exchange switched to an electronic trading system in 1995. It took the exchange only fifty days to make this transition.

3.7.1 About the Bombay Stock Exchange

- **BSE Sensex** or **Bombay Stock Exchange Sensitivity Index** is a value – weighted index composed of 30 stocks that started January 1, 1986.
- **The Bombay Stock Exchange (BSE)** is the oldest Stock Exchange in Asia and has the third largest number of listed companies in the world, with 4900 listed as of Feb 2010.
- It is located at **Dalal Street, Mumbai, India.**
- On Feb, 2010, the equity Market Capitalization of the companies listed on the BSE was US$1.28 trillion, making it the largest stock exchange in South Asia and the 12th largest in the world.
- With over 4900 Indian companies listed & over 7700 scripts on the stock exchange, it has a significant trading volume.
- Though many other exchanges exist, BSE and the National Stock Exchange of India account for most of the trading in shares in India

3.8 NATIONAL STOCK EXCHANGE OF INDIA

The National Stock Exchange of India (NSEI) was established in 1994 to encourage stock exchange reform through system modernisation and competition. It is an electronic screen based system where members have equal access and equal opportunity of business irrespective of their location in different parts of the country as they are connected through a satellite network.

The National Stock Exchange is to operate in two segments as outlined below:

- Wholesale Debt Market
- Capital Market

Wholesale Debt Market is concerned with trading instruments such as Gilt edge securities, commercial papers, PSU Bonds, units, and certificate of Deposits.

The Capital Market is concerned with equity and corporate debt instruments.

3.8.1 Objectives of National Stock Exchange

The NSE objectives as outlined below:

- It establishes nationwide trading facility for equity debt and hybrid.
- It facilitates equal access to investors across the country.
- It provides fairness, efficiency and transparency to the securities trading.
- It enables shorter settlement cycles.
- It meets international securities market standard.

3.8.2 Features of NSE

- It set up a fully automated screen based trading system
- It has consists of three segments: The capital market segment, wholesale debt market segment and derivatives market
- It market is a fully automated screen based environment
- It owns satellite network by through market operates with all participants stationed at their office and making use of their computer terminals, to receive market information, to enter orders and execute to trade.
- When a trade take place, a trade confirmation slip is printed at the trading member's work station. It gives detail like price/quantity, code number of the party and so on.
- It pending orders is delayed, the identity of the trading is not revealed to others.
- On the eighth day of trading, each member get a statement showing his net position as the clearing house of the securities.
- Members are required to deliver securities and cash by the thirteenth and fourteenth day respectively, the fifteenth day is the payout day.
- It automated trade matching system secures the best prices available in the market to the investor.

3.9 CAPITAL MARKET

The capital market is a market for buying and selling of equity, debt and securities. Generally, it deals with long term securities that have a maturity period of above one year. Capital market a market where debt or equity securities are traded.

Debt Definition

Debt means a liability or obligation in the form of bonds, loan notes, or mortgages, owed to another person or persons and required to be paid by a specified date (maturity).

Equity Definition

Equity means:

- Ownership interest in a corporation in the form of common stock or preferred stock.
- It also refers to total assets minus total liabilities, in which case it is also referred to as shareholder's equity or net worth.

3.9.1 Security Definition

An investment instrument, like any note, stock, treasury stock, bond, debenture, certificate of interest or participation in any profit sharing agreement or in any oil, gas, or other mineral royalty or lease, any collateral trust certificate, pre-organisation certificate or subscription, transferable share, investment contract, voting trust certificate, certificate of deposits for a security, any part, call straddle, option or privilege on any security, certificate of deposit, or group or index of securities (including any interest therein or based on the value thereof), or any put call, straddle, option, or privilege entered into on a national securities exchange relating to foreign currency, or in general, any instrument commonly known is a security

3.9.2 Functions of Capital Market

- Policy matters relating to the development and regulation of securities markets and investor protection.
- Policy matters relating to domestic mutual funds, venture capital funds, collective investment schemes etc.
- Organisational matters relating to SEBI and Securities Appellate Tribunal (SAT).
- Policy formulation and approval of External Commercial Borrowing.
- Matters relating to Unit Trust of India.
- Pension Reforms.
- Its responsibility of formulation of suitable policies for the development of capital market in consultation with SEBI, RBI and other agencies.
- Capital market deals with all organisational matters relating to raise funds.
- The capital market works as important source for the productive use of the economy savings.
- It provides incentives to save and facilitates capital formation by offering suitable rates of interest in terms of the price of capital.
- It should provide an avenue for investors, especially for the Household Sector to invest in financial asset that are more productive than physical assets.
- It facilitates increase in production and productivity in the economy. Therefore, it enhances the economic welfare of the society.
- In capital market, the different financial institution operations to influence economic growth.
- A good capital market principally consist of expert intermediaries promotes stability in values of securities representing capital funds.

3.9.3 Features of Indian Capital Market

- Greater reliance on debt instruments as against equity and in particular borrowing from financial institutions.
- Issue of debentures, specifically, convertible debentures with automatic or compulsory conversion into equity without the normal option given to investors.
- Floatation of Mega Issues for the purpose of takeover, amalgamation etc. and avoidance of borrowing from financial institutions for the fear of their discipline and conversion clause by the bigger companies, and this has now become optional.
- Avoidance of underwriting by some companies to reduce the costs and avoid scrutiny by the FIs. It has become optional now.

- Fast growth of mutual funds and subsidiaries of banks for financial services leading to larger mobilisation of savings from the capital market.

3.9.4 Capital Market Structure

Capital market may be classified into three parts:

1. Industrial Securities Market
2. Government Securities Market
3. Long-term Loans Market

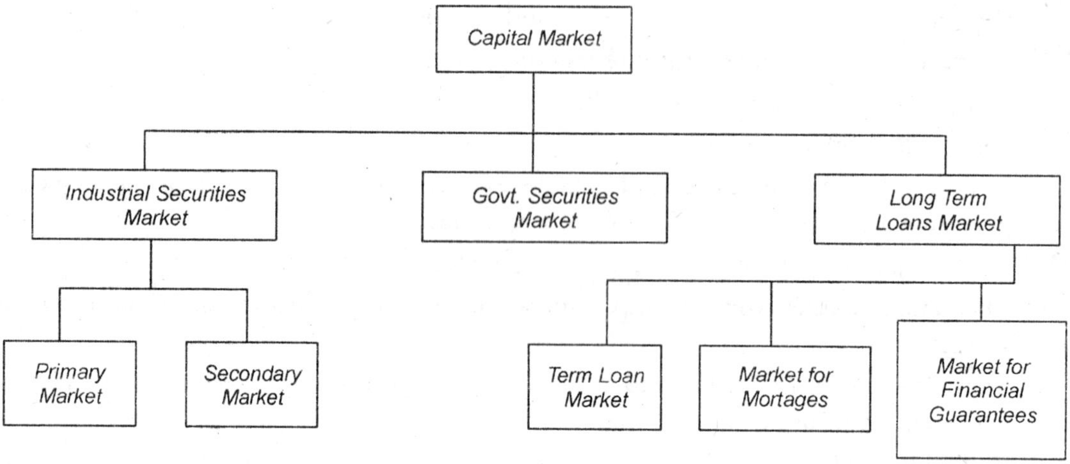

1. Industrial Securities Market

Industrial Securities Market includes industrial securities. They are as mentioned below:

- Equity shares or Ordinary shares
- Preference shares
- Debentures or bonds

Industrial securities market further classified into two types. They are as notified below:

- Primary Market or New Issue Market
- Secondary Market or Stock Exchange

Primary/New Issue Market

Primary market is the market for new securities issues, in the primary market the security is purchased directly from the issuer. This differs from the secondary market. The primary market facilitates capital formation.

A company may raise capital by through primary market. There are three routes to raise capital from the public.

- Public Issue
- Rights Issue
- Private Placement

Secondary Market

Secondary market is a market in which an investor purchases a security from another investor rather than issuer, subsequent to the original issuance in the primary market. It is also called after market. Generally, securities are listed in the stock market and it provides a continuous and regular market for buying and selling of securities. Secondary market has controlled by Securities Contracts (Regulation) Act, 1956.

2. GOVERNMENT SECURITIES MARKET

Government securities market is also called as Gilt-Edged Securities. There are many types of Government Securities that consist of short-term and long-term Government Securities are issued by the Central Government, State Governments, and Semi-Government Authorities. Government Securities are promissory notes, bearer bonds which can be discounted and Treasury bills.

3. Long-term Loans Market

Under this market, Development Banks and Commercial Banks can play a significant role. Because they are supplying long-term loans to corporate customers. Long-term loans may be classified into three types.

They are as outlined below:

- Term Loans Market
- Mortgages Market
- Financial Guarantees Market

3.10 MONEY MARKET

Money market is a market for short term loans or financial assets. It is market for the lending and borrowing of short term funds. It does not actually deal in cash or money.

3.10.1 Features of a Money Market

- It is a market purely for short term funds or financial assets called near money.
- It deals with debt instrument which have a maturity of less than one year at the time of issue are called money market instruments.
- Money market instruments are highly liquid and have negligible risk.
- The money market is dominated by the government, financial institutions, and banks and corporate.
- Money market transactions have to be conducted without help of the brokers.
- It consists of sub-markets, each specialising in a particular type of financing. For example, call money market, acceptance market, bill market and so on.

3.10.2 Objectives of Money Market

- It provides a parking place to employ short term surplus funds
- It provides room for overcoming short term deficits
- It enable to the Central Bank to influence and regulate liquidity in the economy through its intervention in the market
- It provides a reasonable access to users of short term funds to meet their requirement quickly, adequately and at reasonable costs.

3.10.3 Structure of Indian Money Market

The Indian Money Market is divided in to three distinct parts:

- **Organised Sector:** This sector consist RBI, SBI& its Subsidiaries.
- **Unorganised Sector:** This part of the money market consists mahajans, Seth & shroffs.
- **Cooperative Sector:** This part is Intermediary between organised & Unorganised Structure.

3.10.4 Components of Money Market

Therefore, it actually deals with money market instrument like as:

1. Treasury bills
2. Certificates of Deposits (CD)
3. Commercial paper

1. Treasury bills

Treasury bills are the most important money market instrument. They represent short term borrowings of the government. Treasury bill market refers to the market where treasury bills are bought and sold.

Treasury bills are very popular and enjoy a higher degree of liquidity since they are issued by government. Treasury bills are issued only by the RBI on behalf of the government. Treasury bills are issued for meeting temporary government deficits. The Treasury bill rate or the rate of discount is fixed by the RBI from time to time. It is short term maturity and high degree of liquidity and security. Though the yield on Treasury bills is somewhat how, yet they have an appeal for the following reasons:

1. These can be transacted readily and there is a very active in secondary market.
2. Treasury bills have nil credit risk and without risk.

2. Certificates of Deposits

Certificate of Deposits (CDs) refers to short term deposits which are transferable from one party to another. Certificate of Deposits are short term deposit instruments issued by banks and financial institutions to raise sums of money.

Features of Certificate of Deposit

- Document of title to time deposit
- Unsecured negotiable promotes
- Freely transferable by endorsement and delivery
- Issued at discount to face value
- Repayable on a fixed date without grace days
- Subject to stamp duty like the promissory notes.

Advantages of Certificate Deposits

- Certificate of deposits is the most convenient instruments to depositors as they enable their short term surpluses to earn higher return.
- A CDs are generally offered a higher rate of interest than Treasury bills or term deposits.
- CDs are generally offered maximum liquidity.
- CDs are transferable by endorsement and delivery.
- CDs holders can resell his certificate to another.
- CDs are generally risk free.

3. Commercial Paper

A commercial paper is an unsecured promissory note issued with a fixed maturity by a company approved by RBI, negotiable by endorsement and delivery, issued in bearer form and issued at discount on the face value as may be determined by the issuing company.

- Commercial paper is a short term money market instruments.
- It comprises promissory note with a fixed maturity.
- Commercial paper is issued at a discount to face value base and it can also be issued in interest bearing form.
- Commercial paper can be issued directly by a company to investors or through banks/ merchant bankers.
- A commercial paper usually has a maturity period of 90 to 180 days.

Advantages of Commercial Paper

1. **Simplicity:** Simplicity is an obvious advantage of commercial paper. It involves hardly any documentation between the issuer and investor.
2. **Flexibility:** Issuer can issue commercial paper with the maturities tailored to match the cash flow of the company.
3. **Diversification:** A well rated company can diversify its source of finance from banks to short term money markets at somewhat cheaper cost.

4. **High Returns:** The commercial paper provides higher returns to investors than they get from the banking system.
5. **Movement of Funds:** Commercial paper facilitates securitisation of loans resulting in creation of a secondary market for the paper and efficient movement of funds are providing cash surplus to cash deficit entities.

3.11 DEPOSITORY SYSTEM IN INDIA

India has adopted the Depository System for securities trading in which book entry is done electronically and no paper is involved. The physical form of securities is extinguished and shares or securities are held in an electronic form. Before the introduction of the depository system through the Depository Act, 1996, the process of sale, purchase and transfer of securities was a huge problem, and there was no safety at all.

3.11.1 Key Features of the Depository System in India

1. **Multi-Depository System:** The depository model adopted in India provides for a competitive multi-depository system. There can be various entities providing depository services. A depository should be a company formed under the Company Act, 1956 and should have been granted a certificate of registration under the Securities and Exchange Board of India Act, 1992. Presently, there are two depositories registered with SEBI, namely:
   - National Securities Depository Limited (NSDL), and
   - Central Depository Service Limited (CDSL)
2. **Depository services through depository participants:** The depositories can provide their services to investors through their agents called depository participants. These agents are appointed subject to the conditions prescribed under Securities and Exchange Board of India (Depositories and Participants) Regulations, 1996 and other applicable conditions.
3. **Dematerialisation:** The model adopted in India provides for dematerialisation of securities. This is a significant step in the direction of achieving a completely paper-free securities market. Dematerialization is a process by which physical certificates of an investor are converted into electronic form and credited to the account of the depository participant.
4. **Fungibility:** The securities held in dematerialized form do not bear any notable feature like distinctive number, folio number or certificate number. Once shares get dematerialized, they lose their identity in terms of share certificate distinctive numbers and folio numbers. Thus all securities in the same class are identical and interchangeable. For example, all equity shares in the class of fully paid up shares are interchangeable.
5. **Registered Owner/ Beneficial Owner:** In the depository system, the ownership of securities dematerialized is bifurcated between Registered Owner and Beneficial Owner. **According to the Depositories Act**, 'Registered Owner' means a depository whose name is entered as such in the register of the issuer. A 'Beneficial Owner' means a person

whose name is recorded as such with the depository. Though the securities are registered in the name of the depository actually holding them, the rights, benefits and liabilities in respect of the securities held by the depository remain with the beneficial owner. For the securities dematerialized, NSDL/CDSL is the Registered Owner in the books of the issuer; but ownership rights and liabilities rest with Beneficial Owner. All the rights, duties and liabilities underlying the security are on the beneficial owner of the security.

6. **Free Transferability of shares:** Transfer of shares held in dematerialized form takes place freely through electronic book-entry system.

3.11.2 Options

A options agreement is a contract in which the writer of the option grants the buyer of the option the right purchase from or sell to the writer a designated instrument for a specified price within a specified period of time.

The writer grants this right to the buyer for a certain sum of money called the option premium. An option that grants the buyer the right to buy some instrument is called a call option. An option that grants the buyer the right to sell an instrument is called a put option. The price at which the buyer an exercise his option is called the exercise price, strike price or the striking price.

3.11.3 Types of Options

As mentioned earlier, the underlying asset for options could be a spot commodity or a futures contract on a commodity. Another variety is the futures-style option.

An option on spot foreign exchange gives the option buyer the right to buy or sell a currency at a stated price (in terms of another currency). If the option is exercised, the option seller must deliver or take delivery of a currency.

Call Option

A call option gives the option buyer the right to purchase currency Y against currency X, at a stated price X/Y, on or before a stated date. For exchange traded options, one contract represents a standard amount of the currency Y. The writer of a call option must deliver the currency if the option buyer chooses to exercise his option.

Put Option

A put option gives the option buyer the right to sell a currency Y against currency X at a specified price on or before a specified date. The writer of a put option must take delivery if the option is exercised.

Strike Price (also called exercise price)

The price specified in the option contract at which the option buyer can purchase the currency (call) or sell the currency (put) Y against X.

Maturity Date

The date on which the option contract expires is the maturity date. Exchange traded options have standardized maturity dates.

American Option

An option, call or put that can be exercised by the buyer on any business day from initiation to maturity.

European Option

A European option is an option that can be exercised only on maturity date.

3.11.4 Futures

A futures contract is an agreement between two parties to buy or sell an asset at a certain specified time in future for certain specified price. In this, it is similar to a forward contract. However, there are a number of differences between forwards and futures. These relate to the contractual features, the way the markets are organized, profiles of gains and losses, kinds of participants in the markets and the ways in which they use the two instruments.

Derivatives

Derivatives are financial instruments which are derived from bank loans, bonds, currencies, money market instruments, equities and commodities. Futures, options, swaps, warrants, swap options, collars, caps, floors, circuses and scores of other products are collectively known as *derivatives.*

All these constitute tools for the management of risk. Hedging strategies depend on the use of derivatives. Derivatives are used by banks to hedge risks, to gain access to cheaper money and to make profits. Banks undertake fee generating activities that include a variety of commitments and contingent claims that corporations demand. Banks also help customers to cope with financial market volatility by offering various derivative securities services such as forward contracts, futures, swaps and options. These activities do not appear on the balance sheet of banks. The capital requirements for off balance sheet activities are lower.

3.11.5 Characteristics of Derivatives

The three-key characteristics of financial derivatives are:

- Their value is derived from an underlying instrument such as stock index (futures and options based on them), currency or interest rates.
- They are vehicles for transferring risk.
- They are leveraged instruments.

3.11.6 Product, Participants and Functions of Derivatives

Derivative contracts have several variants. The most common are Forwards, Future, Options and Swaps. The following three categories of Participants-Hedgers, Speculators, and Arbitrageurs.

1. **Hedger:** Hedgers face risk associated with the price of an asset. They use futures or options markets to reduce the risk. Thus, they are operation who wants to eliminate the risk composing of their portfolio.

2. **Speculators:** They wish to be on future movements in the price of an asset. A speculator may buy securities in anticipation of rise in price. If this expectation comes true he sells the securities at a higher price and makes a profit. Usually the speculator does not take delivery of securities sold by him. He only receives and pays the difference between the purchase and sale prices.
3. **Arbitrageurs:** They are in business to take advantage of discrepancy between prices in two different markets. If for example, they see the future price of an asset getting out of line with the cash price, they will take off setting positions in two markets to lock in profit.

3.11.7 Types of Derivatives

The most commonly used derivative contract is forwards, futures and options:

1. **Forwards:** A forward contract is a customized contract between two entities, where settlement takes place on a specific date in the futures at today's pre-agreed price.
2. **Futures:** A future contract is an agreement between two parties to buy or sell an asset at a certain time the future at the certain price. Futures contracts are the special types of forward contracts in the sense that are standardized exchange traded contracts.
3. **Options:** It is of two types: call and put options.
   - **Call Option:** It gives an owner the write to buy a specified quantity of the underlying assets at a predetermined price i.e. the exercise price, or the specific date i.e. is the date of maturity.
   - **Put Option:** It gives the holder the right to sell a specific quantity of underlying assets at an agreed price on date of maturity he gets the right to sell.
4. **Leaps:** Normally option contracts are for a period of 1 to 12 months. However, exchange may introduce option contracts with a maturity period of 2-3 years. These long-term option contracts are popularly known as Leaps or Long term Equity Anticipation Securities.
5. **Baskets:** Baskets options are option on portfolio of underlying asset. Equity Index Options are most popular form of baskets.
6. **Swaps:** These are private agreements between two parties to exchange cash flows in the future according to a prearrange formula. They can be regarded as portfolios of forward's contracts. The two commonly used swaps are:

   (i) **Interest Rate Swaps:** These entail swapping both Principal and interest between the parties, with the cash flow in one direction being in a different currency than those in the opposite direction.

   (ii) **Currency Swaps:** These entail swapping both Principal and interest between the parties, with the cash flow in one direction being in a different currency than those in the opposite direction.

3.12 RESERVE BANK OF INDIA

Prior to 1934 many attempts have been made to set up a Central Bank in the country. But such attempts failed to bear any fruit. In 1921 the Government of India established the Imperial Bank of India to serve as the Central Bank of India. But it did not succeed in its functioning as the Central Bank of the country. In 1925, the Hilton Young Commission was appointed by the Government to express the views. It recommended for the establishment of a Brand new Central Bank. In 1929, the Central Banking Enquiry Committee again made a forceful plea for the establishment of the Central Bank for the country. Consequently, RBI Act was passed in1934 and **RESERVE BANK STARTED FUNCTIOING FROM 1st April, 1935.**

It was inaugurated with a share capital of Rs. 5 Crore divided into shares of Rs. 100 each fully paid up. The entire share was firstly owned by private shareholders. The government of India held shares of nominal value of Rs. 2, 22,000.

Central Bank

It occupies a pivotal position in the monetary and banking structure of the country. It is undisputed leader of the money market.

So, it supervises, controls and regulates the activities of the Commercial banks affiliated in country. As the highest monetary institution in the country, it is charged with the duty and responsibility of carrying out the monetary policy by the government.

KISCH AND ELKIN: "The essential function of a central bank is the maintenance of the stability of the monetary standard."

R G HAWTREY: "The essential characteristic of a central bank is its function as the lender of the last resort."

So, it can be defined precisely as "apex banking and monetary institution whose main function is to control, regulate and stabilize the banking and monetary system of the country in the national interests."

3.12.1 Necessity of a Central Bank

1. Control of credit
2. Issue of paper currency
3. Economic help to the commercial banks
4. Implementation of the government's monetary policy

3.12.2 Principal of central Bank

1. The central bank is always inspired by the spirit of national welfare
2. Monetary and financial stability
3. Freedom from political influence
4. No competition with member banks

3.12.3 Function of Central Bank

1. **Monetary Authority:** The Reserve Bank of India Formulates implements and monitors the monetary policy. Its main objective is maintaining price stability and ensuring adequate flow of credit to productive sectors.
2. **Regulator and supervisor of the financial system:** Prescribes broad parameters of banking operations within which the country's banking and financial system functions. Their main objective is to maintain public confidence in the system, protect depositors' interest and provide cost-effective banking services to the public.
3. **Manager of Exchange Control:** The manager of the exchange control department manages the Foreign Exchange Management Act, 1999. His main objective is to facilitate external trade and payment and promote orderly development and maintenance of foreign exchange market in India.
4. **Issuer of currency:** The person who is issuer issues and exchanges or destroys currency and coins not fit for circulation. His main objective is to give the public adequate quantity of supplies of currency notes and coins and in good quality.
5. **Developmental role:** The reserve bank of India performs a wide range of promotional functions to support national objectives. The promotional functions are such as contests, coupons, maintaining good public relations, and many more.
6. **Related Functions:** There are also some of the relating functions to the above mentioned main functions. They are such as Banker to the Government, Banker to banks etc.
7. **Banker to the Government:** performs merchant banking function for the central and the state governments; also acts as their banker.
8. **Banker to banks:** maintains banking accounts of all scheduled banks.
9. **Supervisory functions:** The Reserve Bank act, 1934 and the Banking Regulation act, 1949 have given the RBI wide powers of supervision and control over commercial and co-operative banks, relating to licensing and establishments, branch expansion, liquidity of their asset, management and methods of working, amalgamation, reconstruction, and liquidation. The RBI is authorized to carry out periodical inspections of banks and to call for returns and necessary information from them.
10. **Promotional functions:** With economic growth assuming a new urgency since Independence, the range of the Reserve Bank's functions has steadily widened. The bank now performs a variety of developmental and promotional functions, which, at one time were regarded as outside the normal scope of central banking.

3.13 BANKING SECTOR REFORMS

The first type of reforms mainly based on Narasimhan Committee recommendations and the principals of new liberalized Indian economy.

- Out of the 27 public sector banks (PSBs), 26 PSBs achieved the minimum capital to risk assets ratio (CRAR) of 9 per cent by March 2000. To enable the PSBs to operate in a more competitive manner, the Government adopted a policy of providing autonomous status to these banks, subject to certain benchmarks.
- The Reserve Bank advised banks in February 1999 to put in place an ALM system, effective April 1, 1999 and set up internal asset liability management committees (ALCOs) at the top management level to oversee its implementation. Banks were expected to cover at least 60 per cent of their liabilities and assets in the interim and 100 per cent of their business by April 1, 2000.
- Interest rate deregulation has been an important component of the reform process. The interest rates in the banking system have been largely deregulated except for certain specific classes; these are savings deposit accounts, non-resident Indian (NRI) deposits, small loans up to Rs.2 lakh and export credit.
- In 1994, a Board for Financial Supervision (BFS) was constituted comprising select members of the RBI Board with a variety of professional expertise to exercise 'undivided attention to supervision'. The BFS, which generally meets once a month, provides direction on a continuing basis on regulatory policies including governance issues and supervisory practices. It also provides direction on supervisory actions in specific cases.
- The share of the public sector banks in the aggregate assets of the banking sector has come down from 90 per cent in 1991 to around 75 per cent in 2004. The share of wholly Government-owned public sector banks has declined from about 90 per cent to 10 per cent of aggregate assets of all scheduled commercial banks during the same period. Diversification of ownership has led to greater market accountability and improved efficiency. Current market value of the share capital of the Government in public sector banks has increased manifold and as such, what was perceived to be a bailout of public sector banks by Government seems to be turning out to be a profitable investment for the Government.
- A Board for Regulation and Supervision of Payment and Settlement Systems (BPSS) has also been recently constituted to prescribe policies relating to the regulation and supervision of all types of payment and settlement systems, set standards for existing and future systems, authorize the payment and settlement systems and determine criteria for membership to these systems. Both the Houses of the Parliament have passed the Credit Information Companies (Regulation) Bill, 2004.
- Consolidation in the banking sector has been another feature of the reform process. This also encompassed the Development Financial Institutions (DFIs), which have been providers of long-term finance.

3.14 NARASIMHAN COMMITTEE

The ***Committee on Banking Sector Reforms Committee***8 headed by Mr. M. Narasimhan, it is also known as ***Narasimhan Committee***. The Committee, headed by former Reserve Bank of India governor M Narasimhan, was appointed by the United Front government to review the progress in banking sector reforms. The committee submitted its recommendations to union Finance Minister Yashwant Sinha in November of 1991.

The Committee was required to review the progress in the reforms in the banking sector over the past six years with and to chart a programme on Financial Sector Reforms necessary to strengthen the India's financial system and make it internationally competitive taking into account the vast changes in the international and financial markets, technogical advances. Some of the recommendations offered by the committee are:

Narasimhan Committee recommendations

1. A reduction, phased over five years in the Statutory Liquidity Ratio (SLR) to 25 percent, synchronized with the planned contraction in Fiscal Deficit.
2. A progressive reduction in the Cash Reserve Ratio (CRR).
3. Gradual deregulation of interest rates.
4. All banks to attain Capita Adequacy 8% in a phased manner.
5. Banks to make substantial provisions for bad and doubtful debts.
6. Profitable and reputed banks are permitted to raise capital from the public.
7. Instituting an Assets Reconstruction Fund to which the bad and doubtful debts of banks and Financial Institutions could be transferred at a discount.
8. Facilitating the establishment of new private banks, subject to RBI norms.
9. Banks and financial institutions to classify their assets into four broad groups, viz, Standard, Sub-standard, Doubtful and Loss.
10. RBI to be primarily responsible for the regulation of the banking system.
11. Larger role for Securities Exchange Board of India (SEBI), particularly as a market regulator rather than as a controlling authority.

3.15 FINANCIAL SECTOR REFORM IN INDIA

The period immediately after independence posed a major challenge to the country. Due to centuries of exploitation at the hands of foreign powers, there were very high levels of deprivation in the economy--both social as well as economic. To take up the Herculean task of rapid growth with socio-economic justice, the country adopted the system of planned economic development after independence. Due to paucity of economic resources and limitations of availability of capital for investment, the government also came up with the policy of setting up public enterprises in almost every field.

The fiscal activism adopted by the government resulted in large doses of public expenditures for which not only the revenues of the government were utilized but the government also resorted to borrowing at concessional rates, which kept the financial markets underdeveloped. The growth of fiscal deficit also continued unabated year after year. Complex structure of interest rates was a resultant outcome of this system.

Nationalisation of major commercial banks in the late sixties and early seventies provided the government with virtually the complete control over the direction of the bank credit. The emphasis was mainly on control and regulation and the market forces had very limited role to play.

UNIT-4

E-Banking

4.1 DEFINITION OF E-BANKING

Electronic banking, also known as electronic funds transfer (EFT),is simply the use of electronic means to transfer funds directly from one account to another, rather than by cheque or cash. You can use electronic funds transfer to:

- Have your pay check deposited directly into your bank or credit union checking account.
- Withdraw money from your checking account from an ATM machine with a personal identification number (PIN), at your convenience, day or night.
- Instruct your bank or credit union to automatically pay certain monthly bills from your account, such as your auto loan or your mortgage payment.
- Have the bank or credit union transfer funds each month from your checking account to your mutual fund account.
- Have your government social security benefits check or your tax refund deposited directly into your checking account.
- Buy groceries, gasoline and other purchases at the point-of sale, using a check card rather than cash, credit or a personal check.
- Use a smart card with a prepaid amount of money embedded in it for use instead of cash at a pay phone, expressway road toll, or on college campuses at the library's photocopy machine or bookstores.

What is electronic banking?

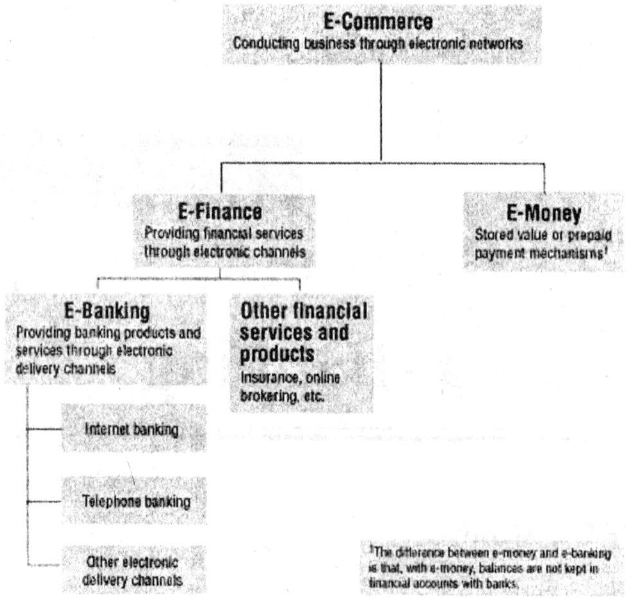

4.1.1 Various Form of E-Banking

Internet Banking

Internet Banking lets you handle many banking transactions via your personal computer. For instance, you may use your computer to view your account balance, request transfers between accounts, and pay bills electronically.

Internet banking system and method in which a personal computer is connected by a network service provider directly to a host computer system of a bank such that customer service requests can be processed automatically without need for intervention by customer service representatives.

Automated Teller Machine (ATM)

An unattended electronic machine in a public place, connected to a data system and related equipment and activated by a bank customer to obtain cash withdrawals and other banking services. Also called automatic teller machine, cash machine; also called money machine.

An **automated teller machine** or **automatic teller machine (ATM)** is an electronic computerized telecommunications device that allows a financial institution's customers to directly use a secure method of communication to access their bank accounts, order or make cash withdrawals (or cash advances using a credit card) and check their account balances without the need for a human bank teller (or *cashier* in the UK). Many ATMs also allow people to deposit cash or cheques, transfer money between their bank accounts, top up their mobile phones' pre-paid accounts or even buy postage stamps.

On most modern ATMs, the customer identifies him or herself by inserting a plastic card with a magnetic stripe or a plastic smartcard with a chip that contains his or her account number. The customer then verifies their identity by entering a pass code, often referred to as a **PIN** (Personal Identification Number) of four or more digits. Upon successful entry of the PIN, the customer may perform a transaction.

The Indian market today has approximately more than 17,000 ATM's.

Tele Banking

Undertaking a host of banking related services including financial transactions from the convenience of customers chosen place anywhere across the GLOBE and any time of date and night has now been made possible by introducing on-line Tele banking services. By dialling the given Tele banking number through a landline or a mobile from anywhere, the customer can access his account and by following the user-friendly menu, entire banking can be done through Interactive Voice Response (IVR) system. With sufficient numbers of hunting lines made available, customer call will hardly fail. The system is bi-lingual and has following facilities offered.

- Automatic balance voice out for the default account.
- Balance inquiry and transaction inquiry in all
- Inquiry of all term deposit accounts
- Statement of account by Fax, e-mail or ordinary mail.
- Cheque book request
- Stop payment which is on-line and instantaneous
- Utility Bill Payments

Smart Card

A smart card usually contains an embedded 8-bit microprocessor (a kind of computer chip). The microprocessor is under a contact pad on one side of the card Think of the microprocessor as replacing the usual magnetic stripe present on a credit card or debit card. Microprocessor on the smart card is there for security. The host computer and card reader actually "talk" to the microprocessor. The microprocessor enforces access to the data on the card.

Smart cards can also be used with a smart card reader attachment to a personal computer to authenticate a user. Smart cards are much more popular in Europe than in the U.S. In Europe the health insurance and banking industries use smart cards extensively. Every German citizen has a smart card for health insurance. Even though smart cards have been around in their modern form for at least a decade, they are just starting to take off in the U.S.

Debit Card

Debit cards are also known as checks cards. Debit cards look like credit cards or ATM (automated teller machine) cards, but operate like cash or a personal check. Debit cards are different from credit cards. While a credit card is a way to "pay later," a debit card is a way to "pay now." When you use a debit card, your money is quickly deducted from your checking or savings account. Debit cards are accepted at many locations, including grocery stores, retail stores, gasoline stations, and restaurants. You can use your card anywhere merchants display your card's brand name or logo. They offer an alternative to carrying a check book or cash.

E-Cheque

- An e-Cheque is the electronic version or representation of paper cheque.
- The Information and Legal Framework on the E-Cheque is the same as that of the paper cheque
- It can now be used in place of paper cheques to do any and all remote transactions.

4.1.2 Benefits of E-Banking

For Banks

Price: In the long run a bank can save on money by not paying for tellers or for managing branches. Plus, it's cheaper to make transactions over the Internet. Customer Base- The Internet allows banks to reach a whole new market and a well off one too, because there are no geographic boundaries with the Internet. The Internet also provides a level playing field for small banks who want to add to their customer base.

Efficiency: Banks can become more efficient than they already are by providing Internet access for their customers. The Internet provides the bank with an almost paper less system.

Customer Service and Satisfaction: Banking on the Internet not only allow the customer to have a full range of services available to them but it also allows them some services not offered at any of the branches. The person does not have to go to a branch where that service may or may not be offer. A person can print of information, forms, and applications via the Internet and be able to search for information efficiently instead of waiting in line and asking a teller. With more better and faster options a bank will surly be able to create better customer relations and satisfaction.

Image: A bank seems more state of the art to a customer if they offer Internet access. A person may not want to use Internet banking but having the service available gives a person the feeling that their bank is on the cutting image.

For Customers

Bill Pay: Bill Pay is a service offered through Internet banking that allows the customer to set up bill payments to just about anyone. Customer can select the person or company whom he wants to make a payment and Bill Pay will withdraw the money from his account and send the payee a paper check or an electronic payment.

Other Important Facilities: E- banking gives customer the control over nearly every aspect of managing his bank accounts. Besides the Customers can, Buy and Sell Securities, Check Stock Market Information, Check Currency Rates, Check Balances, See which checks are cleared, Transfer Money, View Transaction History and avoid going to an actual bank. The best benefit is that Internet banking is free. At many banks the customer doesn't have to maintain a required minimum balance. The second big benefit is better interest rates for the customer.

4.1.3 Concerns with E-Banking

As with any new technology new problems are faced.

Customer support: banks will have to create a whole new customer relations department to help customers. Banks have to make sure that the customers receive assistance quickly if they need help. Any major problems or disastrous can destroy the banks reputation quickly an easily. By showing the customer that the Internet is reliable you are able to get the customer to trust online banking more and more.

Laws: While Internet banking does not have national or state boundaries, the law does. Companies will have to make sure that they have software in place software market, creating a monopoly.

Security: customer always worries about their protection and security or accuracy. There are always questions whether or not something took place.

Other challenges: lack of knowledge from customers end, sit changes by the banks, etc

4.1.4 The Indian Experience of E-banking

India is still in the early stages of E-banking growth and development. Competition and changes in technology and lifestyle in the last five years have changed the face of banking. The changes that have taken place impose on banks tough standards of competition and compliance. The issue here is – 'Where does

India stands in the scheme of E-banking.' E-banking is likely to bring a host of opportunities as well as unprecedented risks to the fundamental nature of banking in India.

The impact of E- Banking in India is not yet apparent. Many global research companies believe that E-banking adoption in India in the near future would be slow compared to other major Asian countries. Indian E-banking is still nascent, although it is fast becoming a strategic necessity for most commercial banks, as competition increases from private banks and non banking financial institutions.

Despite the global economic challenges facing the IT software and services sector, the outlook for the Indian industry remains optimistic.

The Reserve Bank of India has also set up a "Working Group on E-banking to examine different aspects of E-banking. The group focused on three major areas of E-banking i.e.

1. Technology and Security issues
2. Legal issues and
3. Regulatory and Supervisory issues.

RBI has accepted the guidelines of the group and they provide a good insight into the security requirements of E-banking.

1. Technology and Security issues

The importance of the impact of technology and information security cannot be doubted. Technological developments have been one of the key drivers of the global economy and represent an instrument that if exploited well can boost the efficiency and competitively of the banking sector. However, the rapid growth of the Internet has introduced a completely new level of security related problems. The problem here is that since the Internet is not a regulated technology and it is readily accessible to millions of people, there will always be people who want to use it to make illicit gains. The security issue can be addressed at three levels.

The first is the security of customer information as it is sent from the customer's PC to the Web server.

The second is the security of the environment in which the Internet banking server and customer information database reside.

Third, security measures must be in place to prevent unauthorized users from attempting to long into the online banking section of the website.

2. Legal issues

From a legal perspective, security procedure adopted by banks for authenticating users needs to be recognized by law as a substitute for signature. In India, the Information Technology Act, 2000, in section 3(2) provides for a particular technology (viz., the asymmetric crypto system and hash function) as a means of authenticating electronic record. Any other method used by banks for authentication should be recognized as a source of legal risk.

3. Regulatory and Supervisory issues

Regarding the regulatory and supervisory issues, only such banks which are licensed and supervised and have a physical presence in India will be permitted to offer E-banking products to residents of India. With institutions becoming more and more global and complex, the nature of risks in the international financial system has changed. The Regulators themselves who will now be paying much more attention to the qualitative aspects of risk management have recognized this.

Though the Indian Government has announced cyber laws, most corporate are not clear about them, and feel they are insufficient for the growth of E-commerce. Lack of consumer protection laws is another issue that needs to be tackled, if people have to feel more comfortable about transacting online. Taxation of E-commerce transaction has been one of the most debated issues that are yet to be resolved by India and most other countries. The explosive growth of e-commerce has led many executives to question how their companies can properly administer taxes on Internet sales. Without sales tax, online sellers get a price advantage over brick and mortar companies. While ecommerce has been causing loss of tax revenues to the Government, many politicians continue to insist that the Net must remain tax-free to ensure continued growth, and that collecting sales taxes on Net commerce could restrict its expansion. A permanent ban on custom duties on electronic transmissions, international tax rules that are neutral, simple and certain and simplification of state and local sales taxes. The Central Board of Direct Taxes, which submitted its report in September 2001, recommended that e-commerce transaction should be taxed just like traditional commerce.

4.2 CONSUMERISM

Philip Kotler defines Consumerism as **"a social movement seeking to augment the rights and power of the buyer in relation to seller"**. Boyd and Allen that "although often abused as a term, consumerism may be best defined as the dedication of those activates of both public and private organizations which are designed to protect individuals from practices that impinge upon their rights as consumer"

Consumerism, interpreted as a collective endeavour of the consumers to protect their interests, is a manifestation of the failure of the business, including that of the public sector, and the government to guarantee and ensure the rights of the consumers

4.2.1 Consumer Rights

Consumers in the advanced countries, obviously, are much more conscious of their rights than in countries like India. In 1962 President John F. Kennedy, and in 1965 President Johnson emphasized the consumer rights and gave an impetus to consumerism in the U.S.A. and other countries.

Important consumer rights include

1. Right against exploitation by unfair trade practices.
2. Right to protection of health and safety from the goods and services the consumers buy are offered free.
3. Right to be heard if there is any grievance or suggestion.
4. Right to get the genuine grievances redressed.
5. Right to choose the best from a variety of offers.

4.2.2 Utility of Consumerism

Well-organised and dynamic consumerism may be expected to produce the following results:

1. Producers and sellers will not take the consumer for granted. When consumers are strong enough to protect their rights, the business will be compelled unfair trade practices.

2. Consumerism will provide feedback for the business. It will enable the producers to understand consumer needs and wants. This will assist in the more effective implementation of the marketing concept or the social marketing concept, depending upon the nature of consumerism.
3. Consumerism will make the government more responsive to consumer interests, prompt it to take necessary. Measures and make the required institutional arrangements to safeguard consumer rights.

4.2.3 Consumer Protection

For effective consumer protection, a practical response on the part of three parties, for example, the business, the Govt. and the consumer, is essential.

Firstly, the business, comprising the producer and the elements of the distribution channel, has to pay due regards to consumer rights. The producer has an inescapable responsibility to ensure efficiency in production and the quality of output. He should also resist the temptation to charge price in a seller's market. Many a times, the imperfections on the supply side, like hoarding and black marketing. Hence, is socially responsible producer should see to it that whatever is produced reaches the ultimate consumer in time and at responsible prices.

Secondly, the Govt. has to come to the rescue of the helpless consumer to prevent him from being mislead, cheated and exploited. It should also take special care of the vulnerable sections.

Thirdly, consumer should accept consumerism as a mean of asserting and enjoying their rights. Consumerism should succeed in making the business and the Govt. more responsive to the rights of the consumers. Consumerism is a social force to make the business more honest, efficient, responsive and responsible.

4.2.4 Consumer Protection and Consumerism in India

Plight of the Indian Consumer

An examination of the important problem facing the Indian consumer would make clear the need for more effective Govt. intervention and consumer movement to safeguard consumer rights.

The following factors make the plight of the Indian consumer miserable–

1. Short supply of many goods and services, especially of essential items is a very serious problem for the Indian consumer. The demand-supply imbalance has produced also the associated evils of profit earning, hoarding and black marketing towards consumer. Although, the situation has improved as a result of the increase in competition due to liberalization, it is still far from satisfactory.
2. Many products with which consumers in advanced countries are quite familiar are still new to very large segment of the Indian consumers. The unfamiliarity of the consumers

with product features make the sale of substandard, inferior or even defective products easier in India than in advance countries.

3. Due to low literacy levels and unsatisfactory flows, the Indian consumers, by and large, are not conscious of all their rights. This encourages irresponsible business attitudes and tactics.
4. It has been said that the legal process in India is comparatively time-consuming. This discourages the consumers from seeking the redressal of their means of the judicial process.
5. Consumerism in India is not well organized and developed.
6. Though there are a number of laws to safeguard the interests of consumers, they are not effectively implemented and enforced to achieve the objectives.

4.3 SOCIAL RESPONSIBILITY OF BUSINESS

Social responsibility is an ethical or ideological theory that an entity whether it is Government Corporation, organization or individual has a responsibility to society.

Social responsibility means eliminating corrupt, irresponsible or unethical behaviour that might bring harm to the community, its people, or the environment before the behaviour happens.

The shareholders, suppliers of resources, the consumers, the local community and society at large are affected by the way an enterprise functions. Thus a business enterprise should be able to strike a balance between these divergent groups.

4.3.1 Factors affecting Social Responsibility of Business Enterprise

1. **Promoters, Directors and Top Management:** The values and vision of promoters and top management is a key influencing factor.
2. **Stakeholders:** Attitude of various stakeholders like shareholders, creditors, employees etc. also affects the social orientation of a company.
3. **Societal Factors:** Social orientation could also be affected by the expectation of the society from the Corporation. Eg: A resourceful firm located in a poor community may be expected to contribute to the development of education facilities of the locality etc.
4. **Industry and Trade Associations:** They influence the behaviour of firms by establishing professional and ethical codes and norms.
5. **Government and Laws:** Laws to curb corruption, unfair practices etc. and the government's view of social responsibility also acts as an influencing factor.

4.3.2 Arguments for Social Responsibility

1. Society and Business are interdependent.
2. Better environment for Business:
3. Public Image

4. Business has the resources and Power
5. Let Business try Prevention is better than Cure. Social involvement of business would foster a harmonious and healthy relationship between society and business to the mutual benefit of both.
6. Moral Responsibility
7. Citizenship Argument
8. Social responsibility like recycling of waste may have favourable financial effects

4.3.3 Arguments against Social Responsibility

1. **Profit Maximization:** Economic efficiency of business should be the top priority and the sole mission of business. In this situation decisions are controlled by their desire to maximize profits for the shareholders while reasonable complying with law.
2. **Society has to pay the Cost:** Costs of social responsibility will be passed on to the society and eventually it is the society which has to bear them.
3. **Lack of social skills:** Business managers are goods at solving matters relating to business and not very effective at solving social problems as their outlook is primarily economic.
4. **Business has enough Power:** Business already has enough social power and the society should not take any steps which give it more power as it could mould social values.
5. **Social Overhead Costs:** Cost of social responsibility will not immediately benefit the business. Why spend money on an object, benefits of which will be realized only in future.
6. **Lack of accountability:** Businessmen have no direct accountability to the people. Unless the society can develop mechanisms which establish direct lines of social accountability from the business to the public, business must not stay away from social activities.

4.3.4 Social Responsibilities towards different sections

1. **Shareholders:** The primary business of a business is to stay in business. To safeguard the capital of the shareholders and to provide reasonable dividends and returns to its shareholders.
2. **Employees:** The success of the organization depends largely on the morale of the employees. Employee morale depends on employer-employee relationship. The responsibility of the organization to the workers includes:
   - Payment of fair wages
   - Provision of best possible working conditions
   - Establishment of fair work standards

- Provision of labour welfare activities
- Arrangement of proper training of workers.
- Reasonable chances of promotion
- Proper recognition, appreciation etc.
- Installation of an effective grievance handling system

4.4 NEW ECONOMIC POLICY-1991

The new economic policy of India is expected to encourage foreign investments by Indian companies. The curbs on growth, even by mergers and acquisition, have been removed, financing restriction has been based, areas of business opened to private companies have been substantially enlarged and foreign tie up policies have been liberalized.

4.4.1 Features of the New Policy

1. Liberalization.
2. Integration with world economy with.
3. Dismantling of tariff wall.
4. Protection of foreign direct investment.
5. Upgrading the technology of production.
6. Financial stability.
7. Outward looking policies.
8. Deregulation of domestic market.

4.4.2 Components of New Economic policy

1. Short term (immediate stabilization)
2. Correcting the disequilibrium in foreign exchange market through demand reduction.
3. Reform in trade policy
4. Reduction in fiscal deficit
5. Dismantling of barrier to free flow of capital.
6. Medium term structural adjustment:
7. Exchange rate.
8. Trade and industrial policy.
9. Policies concerning the public sector.
10. Financial sector.
11. Capital market.(deregulation of prices and investment, change in structure of taxation & public expenditure, privatization of public enterprise).

Advantages of new economic policy

1. Increase in GDP growth rate
2. Increase in foreign direct investment
3. Increase in foreign exchange
4. Outsourcing

Disadvantages of new economic policy

1. Growing unemployment
2. Neglect of agriculture
3. Growing personal disparities
4. Infrastructural inadequacies
5. Wide spread poverty.
6. Demonstration effect (luxury goods)

4.4.3 Outcome of New Economic policy

- Liberalization
- Privatization
- Globalization

4.4.3.1 Liberalization

It means to free the economy from the direct control of the Govt. before the year 1991, Govt. Had imposed its control on the majority of the Indian Economy like:

- Industrial Licensing System
- Price Control
- Financial control on goods
- Import License
- Foreign Exchange control
- Restrictions on heavy Investments

After the year 1991, the decision was made to lift up the control of Govt. In order to liberalize the economy for the purpose of increasing the growth rate of Indian Economy and to be capable to compete with world economy.

Measure Taken for Liberalization

1. **Abolition of Industrial Licensing and Registration:** Till now the industrial sector including both public and private industries were functioning under a rigid licensing system. But now it was the time to give the industrial policy more relaxations. Industrial licensing was abolished for the almost whole industrial sector except the following industries:

- Liquor
- Cigarette
- Defence Equipments
- Drugs
- Industrial Explosives
- Dangerous chemicals

2. **Concession from Monopolies Act:** At the time of economic reform, the companies having assets more than 100 crores were put under MRTP Act and were facing many restrictions imposed by the Govt. but at the time of Liberalisation all those companies were freed from MRTP Act. Now those companies were free to expand their business and investment limit restrictions were also abolished. Now there was no restriction on the setting up new industries or expansion of industries or taking over and amalgamations.
3. **Freedom for Expansion and Production to Industries:** Under this the companies are not required to take official approval by the Govt. For expansion and production of the business.
4. **Increase in the Investment limit of small industries:** Investment limits for small scale industries was raised to 1 crore for the purpose of adopting the modern technologies.
5. **Freedom to Import capital goods:** After liberalization Indian Industries were freed to buy modernized machineries and raw material from abroad in order to expand their operations of business.
6. **Freedom to Import Technology:** Objective of this new economic policy was to develop the fast growing companies like computers and electronics. Govt. allowed those industries to import high technologies from abroad.
7. **Free determination of Interest Rates:** Reserve Bank of India was not going to control the interest rates of the banking system in India now. This authority was given to all the banks in India that they can increase or decrease the interest rates of borrowings and deposits.
8. **Action plan for Information Technology and Software Development:** Information technology and software development industry submitted 108 points action plan to Indian Govt. which got the recommendation and got approved by the Indian Govt. and orders were issued for the implementation in India at the earliest.

4.4.3.2 Privatization

Privatization means allowing the private sector to set up more and more industries that were previously reserved only for public sector. Under this economy policy many of the existing enterprises of public sector are either wholly or partially sold to private sector.

"Privatisation is the general process of involving the private sectors in the ownership or operation of the state owned enterprises."

Need for Privatization

- Inefficiency of the public sectors.
- Most of the public sectors enterprises were making losses.
- Managers were not free to take the decisions regarding business.
- Biasness of ministers in taking the business decisions.
- Production capacity remained under utilized.
- To compete with the other economies in the world.
- To enhance the quality of production.
- To provide maximum benefits to the consumers.

4.5 GLOBALISATION

It means the expansion of business into other countries. In this, the economy of one country integrates with the economy of other country under the condition of unrestricted free flow of the trade of goods and services, technology, capital, and movement of perssons across the borders.

"Globalisation may be defined as a process associated with increasing openness, growing economic independence and deepening economic integration in the world economy."

4.5.1 Parameter of Globalisation

1. Reduction of trade barriers for free flow of goods and services across border.
2. Creating environment for free flow of capital.
3. Creating environment for free flow of technology.
4. Creating environment for free movement of labour in different countries.

4.5.2 Features of Globalisation

1. Business expands throughout the world.
2. Goods and services are bought and sold from/to any country in the world.
3. Difference between domestic and foreign markets comes to an end.
4. Production are planned and developed according to the target market of whole world.
5. Manufacturing of goods can be made in any part of the world and distribution of those can be made in entire world.
6. Outsourcing of goods and services can be done.

4.5.3 Sources of Globalisation

1. Technological Advancements.
2. Trade Liberalisation.

3. Organizations having wider reach.
4. Global Agreements.
5. Cultural Developments.

4.5.4 Advantages of Globalization

- The advantage of this trade is every country gets several goods and services cheaper from other countries.
- As a result of which instead of paying more for the same goods and services in their own country.
- Now they pay less for the same goods and get them from other countries.
- This results in a higher standard of living.

4.5.5 Disadvantages of Globalization

- Certain industries within a country may not be able to produce those goods and services cheaper than other countries.
- As a result it cannot compete with the foreign market and eventually will have a sudden death.
- Many people within the country may lose jobs and be reduced to destitution.
- Alternative jobs may not be there. As a result their services are lost once and for all.

4.5.6 Process of Globalisation

Globalisation is a process which happens slowly and gradually. It does not take place at once. Normally company has to follow a certain process to be a part of the global market. There are five stages through which an organization can make its place in global market.

Stage-I: Domestic Company exports to foreign country through the dealers and distributors of the home country.

Stage-II: Domestic Company now exports its goods and services to foreign country directly on its own.

Stage-III: Domestic Company establishes its production and marketing operations in various potential countries and becomes an international level company (MNC).

Stage-IV: The Company replicate (becomes almost same) as a foreign company in the foreign country by having all facilities like R&D, full-fledged human resource etc.

Stage-V: The Company becomes a true foreign company as it starts to serve the needs of foreign customers just like the host country's company.

4.5.7 Essential Condition of Globalisation

There are few essential conditions which should be provided by the host country's government for making the Globalisation successful. They are as follows:

- All the tariffs should be removed.
- Freedom should be given to the business and industries.
- Complete freedom to be provided to public sector to compete with private sector.
- Bureaucratic hurdles should be removed.
- Rules & regulations of control are liberalised to encourage globalization.
- Competitiveness should be based on quality, prices, delivery, customer services etc.
- Administrative and Governmental support for making globalization successful.
- Money and capital markets should be developed.

4.5.8 Types/Components of Globalisation

1. **Globalisation of Markets:** Globalisation of markets means integration or merger of the different markets of the world into a single market. Under this situation, there are common norms, values, tastes, preferences and convenience which are observed in this kind of markets.

Features

- Size of the company which is willing to enter into global market does not matter. It is not necessary that only large companies can create global market but small scale industries can also be a part of it.
- Distinction between the Domestic market and Foreign market still prevails/remains depending upon the quality, pricing etc. of the goods manufactured by them.
- Due to this distinction, different strategies are needed for the companies to produce goods and services as good as foreign companies.
- Global firms have to compete with each other in different markets for their survivals.

Reasons for Globalisation of Markets

- Size of domestic market is becoming small for the companies due to increase in the production level of the companies.
- To increase the income of the company and to maximize the profitability of the business.
- Shortage of production as compared to the excessive demand in the country pulled foreign companies to enter into the global markets to fulfill the actual demand of the target market.
- Adverse selling environment regarding any product in the country will push that organization to identify and sell its products in the markets out of their country.
- Expanding business globally this will also help that company to reduce its business risk.

2. **Globalisation of Production:** Globalisation of production means when a company establish its plant or unit in other country to produce some particular product to sell in that particular market. It also happens if the manufacturing facilities of the host country seems to be favourable than the home country.

Features

- To produce good quality of goods and services at low and reasonable cost.
- Economy of that country is favourable for establishing the industry.
- Availability of cheap raw material.
- Availability of cheap labour in underdeveloped countries.

Reasons for Globalisation of Production

- Raw Material availability in bulk/excess in foreign country or underdeveloped countries.
- Availability of skilled and unskilled labour.
- Some countries impose restrictions on imports but on the other hand they allow foreign countries to establish the industry in their country.
- To reduce transportation cost.
- To produce goods and services as per the requirements and preferences of the customers.

3. **Globalisation of Technology:** Under this process the Technological advancement is the only way for the foreign companies to enter into the foreign market and to develop itself into a global company.

4.5.9 Methods of Globalisation of Technology

1. Joint-Ventures and Mergers.
   - **Joint – Ventures:** Partnership of two or more companies of different countries.
   - **Merger:** One company Takeover the other (foreign) company under its ownership.
2. **On the basis of Royalty or Outright Purchase of Technology:** Under this method the companies with higher technologies allows the companies of other countries to adopt their technology on the basis of royalty payments or on outright purchase basis.
3. **Technological Collaboration:** In this method the companies of less developed countries collaborates with the companies of developed countries having advance technologies.
4. **Latest Technology:** Companies with latest technologies obtains advantageous position of producing high quality products at low prices. Due to these advantages, companies enter the foreign markets to earn huge profits.

5. **Globalisation of Investments:** It is also popularly known as Foreign Direct Investments (FDI). All the countries in the world have removed the investment barriers. In India Foreign Direct Investment in some specific sectors is allowed up to 51% out of the total capital share and in almost all other sectors 49% out of the total capital share is allowed as the Foreign Direct Investments.

4.5.10 Reasons for Globalisation of Investments

- Foreign companies go for FDI to avoid the restrictions imposed by the host country on exports.
- MNC's invest in foreign countries to have control over the manufacturing and marketing activities of the business.
- Volume of global trade has increased and it needs the foreign money for further business.
- Some countries imposed the restrictions of licensing which is to be issued only to domestic companies so in case foreign companies enter these markets through FDI.
- Rate of Interest and rate of Returns are high in less developed countries as compared to developed countries.

4.6 EXIM POLICY

EXIM Policy is a set of guide lines and instructions established by DGFT in matters related the import and export of goods in India.

- This policy is regulated by Foreign Trade Development and Regulation Act1992.
- Governing body Directorate General of Foreign Trade.

4.6.1 Objectives of EXIM Policy

- To accelerate the economy
- To provide excess to essential raw material, intermediate, component
- To enhance techno local strength and efficiency of Indian agriculture, industry and services
- To generate new employment
- To encourage the attainment of internationally accepted standards of quality

4.6.2 EXIM Policy (1992-1997)

- Govt. of India for the first time introduced The Indian Exim policy on April -1, 1992.
- First time to bring stability and continuity The Exim Policy was made for the duration five years.
- But the Central Government reserves the right to make any amendments to the trade policy in public interest.
- This policy was thought to be a major step towards the economic reforms of India.

4.6.3 EXIM Policy (1997-2002)

The export and import policy, 1997- 2002 (coinciding with the period of ninth five year plan) sought to consolidate the gains of the previous policy and further carry forward the process of liberalization by deregulating and simplifying procedures and removing quantitative restrictions in a phased manner. It set an ambitious target of attaining an export level of US$ 90-100 billion by the year 2002 and achieving 1 per cent share in world trade.

Objectives

The principal objectives of the policy were the following:

1. To accelerate the country's transition to a globally – oriented vibrant economy to derive maximum benefits from expanding global market opportunities.
2. To stimulate sustained economic growth by providing access to essential raw materials, intermediates, Components, consumables and capital goods required for augmenting production.
3. To enhance the technological strength and efficiency of Indian agriculture, industry and services, thereby improving their competitive strength while generating new employment opportunities, and encourage the attainment of internationally accepted standards of quality.
4. To provide consumers with good quality products at reasonable prices.

Salient Features

Following were the salient features of the policy:

1. Exports and imports shall be free, except to the extent they are regulated by the provisions of this policy.
2. The Central Government may in public, interest, regulate the import or exports of goods by means of a negative list of imports or a negative list of exports, as the case may be.
3. The negative list may consist of goods, the import or export of which is prohibited, restricted through licensing, or canalised.
4. Prohibited items in the Negative list of Imports shall not be imported and prohibited items in the Negative list of exports shall not be exported.
5. Any goods, the export or import of which is restricted through licensing, may be exported or imported only in accordance with a license issued in this behalf.
6. Any goods, the import or export of which is canalised, may be imported or exported by canalising agency specified in the negative list.
7. No export or import shall be made by any person without an importer– exporter code (IEC) number unless specifically exempted.

4.6.4 EXIM Policy (1999-2000)

In its effort to further dismantle the import control regime and hasten the integration of the Indian economy with the world economy, the government announced a revised export-import policy on March 31, 1999 which came into force on Aprill, 1999.

The new export –import policy freed import of 894 items of consumer goods, agricultural products and textile from licensing requirements. In other words a number of Consumer items could now be imported license-free subject only to the payment of import duty. Physical controls on imports were removed and the only control over imports was fiscal in nature, i.e. adjusting import duty to regulate imports. These adjustments were to be made within the upper limit prescribed by WTO.

Moreover, another 414items were removed from the restricted list, allowing these to be imported against special import licenses. India's international commitments require it to remove licensing curbs on imports by the year 2003.

4.6.5 EXIM Policy (2000-2001)

The union commerce and industry minister announced on March 31, 2000 the new export-import policy of the government of India for the year 2000-2001. The export –import policy envisaging a 20 percent export growth in dollar terms in 2000-2001, brought about a major rationalisation in export promotion schemes and launched a series of sector specific initiatives.

Export Promotion: In a major initiative to boost exports, the Government announced the following measures:

Special Economic Zones (SEZ): in the pattern of Chinese models the government announced the setting up of two SEZs at Positra in Gujarat and Nangunery in Tamil Nadu. Industrial units located in SEZs will be exempted from rules and regulations governing exports and imports. The entire production will have to be exported from these zones. Sales from Domestic Tariff Area (DTA) can be done only on full payment of custom duty. Several Export Processing Zones (EPZs)will shortly be converted into SEZs. The EPZs located in Kandla, Vizag and Kochi will be converted into SEZs immediately. It was further announced that 100 percent foreign direct investment (FDI) would be allowed in all products in SEZs.

SEZs would be treated as if they are outside the customs territory of the country. The units would be able to import capital goods and raw material duty free. The movement of goods to and from SEZs would be unrestricted.

It is noteworthy that SEZs have played a crucial role in boosting China's exports and presently the country derives 40 percent of its exports from such zones. However, Chinese SEZs are based on contract labour system (hire and fire policy). The commerce minister while announcing the EXIM policy categorically ruled out any changes in labour laws. Moreover, there is no system of reservation of items for small scale industries in China. It is unclear if the Government of India would allow the production of reserved item for small industries in the SEZs. Still further there are various infrastructural bottlenecks like power shortage, lack of transport facility and of course procedural delays. Hence the success of SEZs in India is a moot question

Sector-Specific Packages: The Export-import policy 2000-2001 announced sector-specific packages for sever core areas to boost export, viz. Gems and jewellery, pharmaceuticals, agrochemicals, biotechnology, silk, leather and garments.

For the gems and jewellery exporters, the government announced a diamond-dollar account (DDA) scheme export proceeds can be retained in a dollar account and the exporters can use funds in this account for import of rough diamonds.

For agrochemicals, biotechnology and pharma units (considered as knowledge-intensive), the government has allowed duty free imports of laboratory equipment, chemicals and reagents up to 1% of the FOB value of exports. Similarly the government increased duty free import of trimmings, embellishments and other items from 2 to 3% of the total export value

Involvement of State Governments in Export Promotions: Since the stages forgo taxes (mainly sales tax) on exports, they have little incentive to promote exports. [1] the 2000-2001 export -import policy announced financial incentives to states based on their export performance. An incentives scheme with an initial outlay of Rs. 250 crores to secure states involvement in the national export drive was unveiled. The states can use the funds for export promotions activities such as infrastructure development. The commerce and industry minister said that he would request the state to treat all units exporting more than 50 percent of their turnover as public utility services. This would enable them to keep their international commitment on delivery schedule.

Furthermore, the minister observed that the recent spectacular growth of software exports was, apart from India's knowledge in high-tech, due to hands off policy of government towards this sector .A similar approach to hardware electronics is called for.

Import liberalisation: The export import policy 2000 to 2001 lifted quantitative restrictions on 714 commonly used items (agricultural products and consumer durables) which can now be freely imported.

Thus, commodities like meat, milk powder, coffee, tea, fish, pickles, cigars , cigarettes, television , radio , tape recorders , foot wares & umbrellas can be imported freely from April 1, 2000. However most of these items will attracts peak rates of basic import duty.

The lifting of licensing and quota restrictions on 714 import items was in line with India's WTO obligations. The government promised to abolish licensing and quota curbs on the remaining 715 items (such liquor, cars etc) in April 2001.

Many critics of new policy fear that that removal of licensing and quota restriction will lead to surge in imports of these items, hurting the domestic industry. However, it is noteworthy that import restrictions are being phased out since 1966 but no extraordinary growth has occurred in the import of freed items. The commerce minister maintains that antidumping and anti-subsidy tariffs and other safeguards would be used if there is sudden search in imports, causing serious injuries to the domestic industry.

4.6.6 EXIM Policy, (2001-2002)

The union commerce and industry minister unveiled on March 31, 2001, the export –import policy for the year 2001-2002.

Removal of Quantitative restrictions: The process of removal of import restrictions, which began in 1991, was completed in a phased manner bye the Export-Import Policy 2001-2002 with the removal of restriction on the remaining of 715 items. This was in tune with the commitments made to the WTO. Out of these 715 items 342 were textile products, 147 were agricultural products and 226 were other manufactured products.

However, import of agricultural products like wheat, rice, maze, copra and coconut oil was placed in the category safe trading. The nominated state trading enterprise will conduct the import of this commodity solely as per commercial consideration. Similarly, import of petroleum products including petrol, diesel &

ATF was placed in the category of state trading in all 27 out of 715 items taken of the quantitative restrictions list were put under the state trading category.

The minister was confident that the Indian market will not swamped by imported brands of commonly used articles. To prevent dumping, government will take recourse to anti-dumping duties and other non-tariff barriers. Arrangements have been made to track, collate and analyse data on 300 sensitive items which mainly comprise farm goods and items produced by small scale sectors.

Agricultural Export Zones: With a view to boost agricultural exports and provide remunerative returns to the farming community, the Export- Import policy proposed the setting up of agricultural export zones. Three such zones are proposed to be set up in himanchal Pradesh, jammu Kashmir (to promote export of apples) and Maharashtra. Government will make efforts to provide improved access to the produce/products of the agriculture and allied sectors in the international market. State governments have been asking to identify product specific agricultural export zones for development for export of specific products from a geographically contiguous area.

4.6.7 EXIM Policy (2002-2007)

The EXIM Policy 2002-07 was unveiled on March 31, 2002. The policy entailed several institutional, infrastructural and fiscal measures intended to promote exports which are conductive to the economic development of the country. The following were the salient features of the policy.

Special Economic zones (SEZs): Offshore banking units (OBUs) were permitted in SEZs. Units in SEZ were permitted to undertake hedging of commodity price risks, provided such transactions are undertaken by the units on stand-alone basis. This will impart security to the returns of the unit.

It has also been decided to permit external commercial borrowings (ECBs) for tenure of less than three years in SEZs. The detailed guidelines will be worked out by RBI. This will provide opportunities for accessing working capital loan for these units internationally competitive rates.

Employment Generation: In an effort to generate additional employment , the following announcements were made pertaining to agricultural and small industry sectors.

Exports restrictions like registration and packaging requirement were removed forthwith on butter, wheat & wheat products, coarse grains groundnuts oil and cashew to Russia. Quantitative and packaging restrictions on wheat and its products, butter, pulses, grains and flour of barley, maize, bajra, ragi and jowar had already been removed on March 5, 2002.

- Restrictions on export of all cultivated varieties of seed, except jute and onion, were removed.
- To promote export of agriculture and agriculture-based products, 20 agriculture export zones were notified.
- In order to promote diversification of agriculture, transport subsidy shall be available for export of fruits, vegetables, floriculture, poultry and dairy products.
- 3 percent special DEPB rate was announced for primary and processed foods exported in retail packaging of 1 kg or less
- An amount of Rs 5 crore under Market Access Initiative (MAI)
- Was earmarked for promoting cottage sector exports coming under te KVIC.
- The units in the handicrafts sector can also access funds from MAI scheme for development of website for visual exhibition of their product.
- Under the export of Promotion Capitals Goods (EPCG) scheme, these units will not be required to maintain average level of exports, while calculating the export obligation.
- These units shall be entitled to the benefit of Export House Status on achieving lower average export performance of Rs 5 crore as against Rs 15 crore for others.
- The units in handicraft sector will be entitled to duty free imports of an enlarged list of items as embellishments up to 3 percent of FOB value of their exports.
- With a view to encouraging further development of centers of economics and export excellence such as Tirupur for hosiery, woollen blanket in Panipat, wollen knitwear in Ludhiana.

Following Benefits Shall be Available to Small Scale Sector

1. Common service providers in these areas shall be entitled for facility of EPCG scheme.
2. The recognized associations of units in these areas will be able to access the funds under the Market Access initiative scheme for creating focused technological services and marketing abroad.

3. Such areas will receive priority for assistance for identified critical infrastructure gaps from the scheme on Central Assistance to States.
4. Entitlement for Export House Status at Rs 15 crore for others.

4.6.8. EXIM Policy (2003-2004)

It had the following provisions

- The policy provided a massive thrust to export of services by introducing duty free export facility for the service sector units having a minimum foreign exchange earning of Rs 10 lakh.
- Encouragement of corporate sector with proven credential to sponsor Agri-Export Zones for boosting farm exports.
- EPCG scheme made more flexible and attractive so that even the small scale sector could set up and expand its manufacturing base for exports.
- Fixing of input-output norms for status holders on priority basis within a period of 60 days and permission to status holders in Software Technology Parks India (STPI) for free movement of professional equipments.
- Simplification and codification of rules, regulations and procedures application on SEZ and EOU units by putting all these rules and regulations in one place, thus greatly facilitating both potential investors and existing units.
- To increase the overall competitiveness of export clusters, a scheme for up gradation of infrastructure in existing clusters/industrial locations would be implemented.
- Extension of Duty Free Replenishment Certificate (DFRC)scheme to deemed exports and reduction in its value addition norms from 33 percent to 25 percent.

4.6.9 EXIM Policy of India (2004-09)

Introduction

1. The foreign trade of India is guided by the Export-Import policy of the Government of India.
2. Regulated by The Foreign Trade Development and Regulation Act 1992.
3. EXIM policy contains various policy decisions with respect to import and exports from the country.
4. EXIM Policy is prepared and announced by the central government.
5. EXIM Policy of India aims to developing export potential, improving export performance, encouraging foreign trade and creating favourable balance of payment position.

About the Policy

1. Mr. Kamal Nath minister for commerce and industry announced this policy on 31st Aug 2004.

2. The duration of the policy is from 1st Sept. 2004 to 31st March 2009.
3. It takes an integrated view of the overall development of India's foreign trade.
4. Aim of the policy is to double the global merchandise trade within the policy time period of 5 years

General Objectives of EXIM Policy

1. To establish the framework for globalization.
2. To promote the productivity competitiveness of Indian Industry.
3. To encourage the attainment of high and internationally accepted standards of quality.
4. To augment export by facilitating access to raw material, intermediate, components, consumables and capital goods from the international market.
5. To promote internationally competitive import substitution and self-reliance.
6. To double our percentage of share of global merchandise trade within the five year.
7. To act as an effective instrument of economic growth by giving a thrust to employment generation.

Highlights of the New Foreign Trade Policy 2004-2009

1. **Special Focus Initiatives:** Semi-urban and Rural Area.
2. **Agriculture:** Vishesh Krishi Upaj Yojana and Agri Export Zones.
3. **Handlooms and Handicrafts:** Mark under Market Access Initiatives Scheme and Proposed to start new SEZ.
4. **Gems and Jewellery:** Import of gold of 18 carat and above has been permitted under the replenishment scheme.
5. **Leather and Footwear:** Duty free import entitlement of specified items shall be 5% of FOB value of exports during the preceding year.
6. Export Promotion Schemes
   - Assistance to States for Infrastructure Development of Exports [ASIDE]
   - Market Access Initiative [MAI]
   - Marketing Development Assistance [MDA]
   - Towns of Export Excellence
   - Target plus Scheme.
   - Served from India Scheme
   - Service Export Promotion Council
7. New Status Holder Categorization Category Total Performance (In Rs.)
   - One Star Export House 15 crore
   - Two Star Export House 100 crore

- Three Star Export House 500 crore
- Four Star Export House 1500crore
- Five Star Export House 5000 Crore

8. **Board of Trade:** The role is to advising government on relevant issues connected with Foreign Trade Policy.

4.7 FOREIGN DIRECT INVESTMENT

Foreign direct investment is that investment, which is made to serve the business interests of the investor in a company, which is in a different nation distinct from the investor's country of origin.

The parent enterprise through its foreign direct investment effort seeks to exercise substantial "*Control*" over the foreign affiliate company.

Exp. - An American company taking a majority stake in a company in India.

FDI flows should get, in the recipient country, reflected in

1. Capital formation
2. Formation of new firms and factories
3. Increase in foreign equity holding in the existing firms
4. Mergers and acquisitions of existing firms and factories

4.7.1 Types of FDI

1. **Greenfield investment:** direct investment in new facilities or the expansion of existing facilities. Greenfield investments are the primary target of a host nation's promotional efforts because they create new production capacity and jobs, transfer technology and know-how, and can lead to linkages to the global marketplace. However, it often does this by crowding out local industry; multinationals are able to produce goods more cheaply (because of advanced technology and efficient processes) and uses up resources (labour, intermediate goods, etc). Another downside of greenfield investment is that profits from production do not feed back into the local economy, but instead to the multinational's home economy. This is in contrast to local industries whose profits flow back into the domestic economy to promote growth.
2. **Mergers and Acquisitions:** occur when a transfer of existing assets from local firms to foreign firms takes place, this is the primary type of FDI. Cross-border mergers occur when the assets and operation of firms from different countries are combined to establish a new legal entity. Crossborder acquisitions occur when the control of assets and operations is transferred from a local to a foreign company, with the local company becoming an affiliate of the foreign company. Unlike Greenfield investment, acquisitions provide no long term benefits to the local economy– even in most deals the owners of the local firm are paid in stock from the acquiring firm, meaning that the money from the sale could never reach the local economy. Nevertheless, mergers and acquisitions

are a significant form of FDI and until around 1997, accounted for nearly 90% of the FDI flow into the United States.

3. **Horizontal Foreign Direct Investment:** is investment in the same industry abroad as a firm operates in at home.

4.7.2 Features of FDI

1. **Stimulation of national economy:** FDI is thought to bring certain benefits to national economies. It can contribute to Gross Domestic Product (GDP), Gross Fixed Capital Formation (total investment in a host economy) and balance of payments. There have been empirical studies indicating a positive link between higher GDP and FDI inflows (OECD a.), however the link does not hold for all regions, e.g. over the last ten years FDI has increased in Central Europe whilst GDP has dropped. FDI can also contribute toward debt servicing repayments, stimulate export markets and produce foreign exchange revenue. Subsidiaries of Trans-National Corporations (TNCs), which bring the vast portion of FDI, are estimated to produce around a third of total global exports. However, levels of FDI do not necessarily give any indication of the domestic gain (UNCTAD 1999). Corporate strategies e.g. protective tariffs and transfer pricing can reduce the level of corporate tax received by host governments. Also, importation of intermediate goods, management fees, royalties, profit repatriation, capital flight and interest repayments on loans can limit the economic gain to host economy. Therefore the impact of FDI will largely depend on the conditions of the host economy, e.g. the level of domestic investment/ savings, the mode of entry (merger & acquisitions or Greenfield (new) investments) and the sector involved, as well as a country's ability to regulate foreign investment (UNCTAD 1999).
2. **Stability of FDI:** FDI inflows can be less affected by change in national exchange rates as compared to other private sources (portfolio investments or loans). This is partly because currency devaluation means a drop in the relative cost of production and assets (capital, goods and services) for foreign companies and thereby increases the relative attraction of a "host" country. FDI can stimulate product diversification through investments into new businesses, so reducing market reliance on a limited number of sectors/products (UNCTAD 1999). However, if international flows of trade and investment fall globally and for lengthy periods, then stability is less certain. New inflows of FDI are especially affected by these global trends, because it is harder for a foreign company to de-invest or reverse from foreign affiliates as compared to portfolio investment. Companies are therefore more likely to be careful to ensure they will accrue benefits before making any new investments. Examples of regional stability are mixed, whilst FDI growth continued in some Asian countries e.g. Korea and Thailand, during the 1996/97 crisis, it fell in others e.g. Indonesia. During Latin America's financial crisis in the 80's many Latin American countries experienced a sharp fall in FDI (UNGA 1999),

suggesting that investment sensitivity varies according to a country's particular circumstances.

3. **Social development:** FDI, where it generates and expands businesses, can help stimulate employment, raise wages and replace declining market sectors. However, the benefits may only be felt by small portion of the population, e.g. where employment and training is given to more educated, typically wealthy elites or there is an urban emphasis, wage differentials (or dual economies) between income groups will be exacerbated (OECD a). Cultural and social impacts may occur with investment directed at non-traditional goods. For example, if financial resources are diverted away from food and subsistence production towards more sophisticated products and encouraging a culture of consumerism can also have negative environmental impacts. Within local economies, small scale and rural businesses of FDI host countries there is less capacity to attract foreign investment and bank credit/loans, and as a result certain domestic businesses may either be forced out of business or to use more informal sources of finance (ECOSOC 2000).
4. **Infrastructure development and technology transfer:** Parent companies can support their foreign subsidiaries by ensuring adequate human resources and infrastructures are in place. In particular "Greenfield" investments into new business sectors can stimulate new infrastructure development and technologies to host economies. These developments can also result in social and environmental benefits, but only where they "spill over" into host communities and businesses (ECOSOC 2000). Investment in research & development (R&D) from parent companies can stimulate innovation in production and processing techniques in the host country. However, this assumes that in-house investment (in R&D, production, management, personnel training) will result in improvements. Foreign technology/organisational techniques may actually be inappropriate to local needs, capital intensive and have a negative affect on local competitors, especially smaller business that are less able to make equivalent adaptions. Similarly external changes in suppliers, customers and other competing firms are not necessarily an improvement on the original domestic-based approaches (UNCTAD 1999).
5. **"Crowding in" or "Crowding out":** "Crowding in" occurs where FDI companies can stimulate growth in up/down stream domestic businesses within the national economies. Whilst "Crowding out" is a scenario where parent companies dominate local markets, stifling local competition and entrepreneurship. One reason for crowding out is "policy chilling" or "regulatory arbitrage" where government regulations, such as labour and environmental standards, are kept artificially low to attract foreign investors, this is because lower standards can reduce the short term operative costs for businesses in that country. Exclusive production concessions and preferential treatment to TNCs by host governments can both restrict other foreign investors and encourage oligopolistic (quasi-monopoly) market structure (ECOSOC 2000, UNCTAD 1999). Empirical data

for these scenarios is variable, but crowding out is thought to be more common in specific sectors. For example, in industries where demand or supply for a product or service is highly price elastic (market sensitive) and capital intensive. Hence regulation brings additional costs of compliance and is therefore much more likely to influence a company's decision to invest in that country.

6. **Scale and pace of investment**: It may be difficult for some governments, particularly low income countries, to regulate and absorb rapid and large FDI inflows, with regard to regulating the negative impacts of large-scale production growth on social and environment factors (WWF 1999). Also a high proportion of FDI inflows in developing economies are commonly aimed at primary sectors, such as petroleum, mining, agriculture, paper-production, chemicals and utilities. Primary sectors are typically capital and resource intensive, with a greater threshold in economies of scale and therefore slower to produce positive economic "spill over" effects (OECD a). Thus, in the short term, low income economies will have less capacity to mitigate environmental damages or take protective measures, imposing greater remediation costs in the long term, as well as potentially irreversible environmental losses (WWF 1999, OECD b).

Why Do Countries want FDI

There are strong reasons why MNCs are welcomed to invest in foreign countries.

1. **FDI is seeks to fill the gaps in technology managerial skills and entrepreneurism:** as a way of filling in gaps between the domestically available supplies of savings, foreign exchange, government revenue, and human capital skills and the desired level of these resources necessary to achieve growth and development targets. The MNCs not only provide financial resources and new factories, but also supply a "package" of needed resources, including managerial experience of training programs to and educate local managers to establish contacts with foreign countries. They bring sophisticated technological knowledge about production processes while transferring modern technology.
2. **Factories set up by MNCs act as nucleuses of growth:** The industry of MNCs gives birth to several other enterprises which would supply inputs to the parent company. It is not that only a few surrounding firms are the beneficiaries.
3. **FDI can generate healthy competition in the recipient countries:** When FDI assumes the form of green field projects, the result is the creation on new enterprises, adding to the number of players in the market. This can increase the level of competition in a host country. It brings consumers choice, tends to bring down prices and shall boost economic welfare of consumers.
4. **Too often location advantages attract FDI:** The location- specific advantages in particular, include natural resources such as oil and other minerals, cost and skill of labours, which are by nature specific to certain locations.

5. **FDI often depends on a country's political attempts to reduce security risks:** For example China state owned petroleum companies have been investing abroad so as to minimize its dependence on foreign companies for oil supplies. The move may also help China hold down prices on the petroleum it receives.
6. **It is the poor countries that deserve FDI more than any others:** Poverty is prevalent, not withstanding globalisation, world becoming flat and millennium agenda. To alleviate poverty they get aid from international institutions and rich countries can be temporary measures. The Economic growth ushered in by increased investment can be a permanent solution.

4.7.3 Factors Influencing FDI

Several factors influence the decision relating to the flow of FDI. These can be classified into three categories,

1. Supply Factors
2. Demand Factors
3. Government Factors
4. **Supply Factors:** Supply factors include production costs, logistics, resource availability and access to technology. These factors influence a firm's decision relating to FDI.
   (i) **Production costs:** Firms seek competitive advantage through low production cost. MNCs locate production facilities in low wage countries. It is just not low labour cost. A host of other factors also figure in low cost, e.g. lower real estate prices, lower taxes, and advantages of low wages and similarly local incentives were the main motive behind establishing industries.
   (ii) **Logistics:** MNCs seek to invest on subsidiaries in foreign markets, if the cost of shipping raw material is high. Coke and PEPSI have set up bottling plants in India as the cost of transporting water from the US is considerable. International businesses also often make investments n host countries to reduce distribution costs. The liberalisation of Latin American markets brought a surge of foreign direct investment in transportation and physical distribution, and foreign providers have upgraded the region's transportation and warehousing facilities.
   (iii) **Natural Resources:** MNCs tend to utilize FDI to access natural resources that are critical to them. Natural resources attract many companies into international markets. To access cheaper energy resources used in manufacturing, several Japanese firms are relocating production to China, Mexico and Vietnam where energy costs are lower.
   (iv) **Key Technology**: Technology and business have been intertwined since the industrial revolution. The connection between the two became even stronger in the information age, particularly with the advent of electronic business exchanges.

Technology influences every aspect of global market places driving innovation, affecting partnerships and locations, and changing business-stakeholder relationships.

2. **Demand Factors:** Market expansion is another motive behind FDI. They include as the following.
   (i) **Customer Access:** Certain international business need to be physically present in foreign markets to serve customers better. KFC cannot provide freshly fried chicken to customers in INDIA from its restaurants in the US. So they want to at customer access.
   (ii) **Competitive Advantage:** A company enjoying great reputation may seek to establish subsidiaries in overseas countries to encase on its brand equity. An owner of a valuable trade mark, brand name, or technology may choose to operate in foreign countries rather than export to them.
   (iii) **Follow the Clients:** Often, clients of a company attract FDI. If one of the clients builds a foreign facility, the company may decide to locate a new factory of its own nearby, thus enabling it to continue to supply its customer promptly and attentively. This practice of "following clients" is likely to be followed in industries in which many component parts are obtained from suppliers with whom the company has a close working relationship.
   (iv) **Follow the Rivals:** Competitor analysis indicates geographic strengths and weakness of individual rivals. From such analysis, firms an select markets for investment. MNCs will be routinely monitoring market sizes and growth rates in over 150 countries. Large and medium-sized growth markets are always attractive propositions, and firms compete to build up factories in these regions and countries such as INDIA, BRAZIL and CHINA.
3. **Government / Political Factors:** Political factors are often the determinants of the quantum and direction of FDI. They are as follows.
   (i) **Economic priorities:** The Economic priorities of developing countries often clash with profit motives of MNCs seeking to invest in such markets. In other words, developing countries want MNCs to invest in infrastructure development area but the international businesses seek to invest in consumer goods industries. Obviously developing countries impose restrictions on the flow of FDI into their economies. Inward flow of FDI was perceived essential as a means of acquiring technology that was not available through licensing agreements and capital goods imports.
   (ii) **Avoidance of Trade Barriers:** In the host country there must be avoidance of Trade barriers to locate the companies. E.g. Fuji photo Film Company that invested $200 million to set up a manufacturing plant in US earlier to this, the company supplied film to its US customers from its factories in the Netherlands and Japan.

While thus exporting to the US, Fuji was paying 3.7% tariff imposed by the US government. This tax has been saved by producing film in the US itself.

(iii) **Development Incentives:** Many governments offer attractive incentives- may, throw red carpet welcome to MNCs to invest in their economies, particularly the developing countries. The theories of FDI explained earlier explain the reasons why developing countries invite FDI. The primary motive to attract FDI is to fill the resource gaps which exist in industrializing countries.

4.7.4 FDI in India

Foreign direct investment in India:

Liberalization of the Indian economy in the early 1990s boosted the inflow of Foreign Direct Investments (FDI) to India. It also helped to open Indian markets to foreign direct investment. Further the government of India simplified the procedures for foreign direct investment in the country in order to encourage the foreign investors to invest in the country. Foreign direct investment in India, came from non resident Indians, international companies, and other foreign investors. FDI inflows to India grew significantly over the years and assumed significant proportions by 2006-2007.

Sectors attracting FDI inflows in India during 2006- 2007 are:

- Real estate
- Construction activities
- Services sector
- Telecommunications
- Electrical equipments that includes electronics and computer software

Countries contributing to FDI inflows in India during 2006- 2007 are:

- USA
- Singapore
- UK
- Netherlands
- Mauritius

In 2006-07, FDI comprised 2.31% of the GDP of India. This was merely 0.77% in 2003-04. FDI comprised 6.42% of total investments in India in 2006-07 which was a significant growth 2.55% in 2003-04. The remarkable growth of FDI in India during 2006-07 had major impacts on the economic growth of the country boosting output and employment significantly. The rapid growth of the economy, favourable investment regime, liberal policy changes and procedural relaxations, has resulted in a horde of global corporations investing in India. The generous inflow of FDI is playing a significant role in the economic growth of the country.

In 2007-08, India's FDI touched US$ 25 billion, up 56 per cent against US$ 15.7 billion in 2006-07, and the country's foreign exchange reserves had crossed US$ 341 billion as on May 21, 2008. In 2005-06, the growth was even sharper at 184 per cent, up from US$ 5.5 billion in 2004-05. Projections say that the country will attract US$ 35 billion in FDI in 2008-09 (as per data released by the Ministry of Commerce and Industry).

Investment in India - Investing in India – Venturing into the Indian Market Investment in Indian market

India, among the European investors, is believed to be a good investment despite political uncertainty, bureaucratic hassles, shortages of power and infrastructural deficiencies. India presents a vast potential for overseas investment and is actively encouraging the entrance of foreign players into the market. No company, of any size, aspiring to be a global player can, for long ignore this country which is expected to become one of the top three emerging economies.

Success in India

Success in India will depend on the correct estimation of the country's potential, underestimation of its complexity or overestimation of its possibilities can lead to failure. While calculating, due consideration should be given to the factor of the inherent difficulties and uncertainties of functioning in the Indian system. Entering India's marketplace requires a well-designed plan backed by serious thought and careful research. For those who take the time and look to India as an opportunity for long-term growth, not short-term profit- the trip will be well worth the effort.

Market potential

India is the fifth largest economy in the world (ranking above France, Italy, the United Kingdom, and Russia) and has the third largest GDP in the entire continent of Asia. It is also the second largest among emerging nations. (These indicators are based on purchasing power parity.) India is also one of the few markets in the world which offers high prospects for growth and earning potential in practically all areas of business. Yet, despite the practically unlimited possibilities in India for overseas businesses, the world's most populous democracy has, until fairly recently, failed to get the kind of enthusiastic attention generated by other emerging economies such as China.

Lack of Enthusiasm Among Investors

The reason being, after independence from Britain 50 years ago, India developed a highly protected, semi-socialist autarkic economy. Structural and bureaucratic impediments were vigorously fostered, along with a distrust of foreign business. Even as today the climate in India has seen a sea change, smashing barriers and actively seeking foreign investment, many companies still see it as a difficult market. India is rightfully quoted to be an incomparable country and is both frustrating and challenging at the same time. Foreign investors should be prepared to take India as it is with all of its difficulties, contradictions and challenges.

Infrastructural hassles

The rapid economic growth of the last few years has put heavy stress on India's infrastructural facilities. The projections of further expansion in key areas could snap the already strained lines of transportation unless massive programs of expansion and modernization are put in place. Problems include power demand shortfall, port traffic capacity mismatch, poor road conditions (only half of the country's roads are surfaced), low telephone penetration (1.4% of population).

Indian Bureaucracy

Although the Indian government is well aware of the need for reform and is pushing ahead in this area, business still has to deal with an inefficient and sometimes still slow-moving bureaucracy.

Diverse Market

The Indian market is widely diverse. The country has 17 official languages, 6 major religions, and ethnic diversity as wide as all of Europe. Thus, tastes and preferences differ greatly among sections of consumers.

Therefore, it is advisable to develop a good understanding of the Indian market and overall economy before taking the plunge. Research firms in India can provide the information to determine how, when and where to enter the market. There are also companies which can guide the foreign firm through the entry process from beginning to end –performing the requisite research, assisting with configuration of the project, helping develop Indian partners and financing, finding the land or ready premises, and pushing through the paperwork required.

4.7.5 Advantages of FDI

1. **Economic growth:** This is one of the major sectors, which is enormously benefited from foreign direct investment. A remarkable inflow of FDI in various industrial units in India has boosted the economic life of country.
2. **Trade:** Foreign Direct Investments have opened a wide spectrum of opportunities in the trading of goods and services in India both in terms of import and export production. Products of superior quality are manufactured by various industries in India due to greater amount of FDI inflows in the country.
3. **Employment and skill levels:** FDI have also ensured a number of employment opportunities by aiding the setting up of industrial units in various corners of India.
4. **Technology diffusion and knowledge transfer:** FDI apparently helps in the outsourcing of knowledge from India especially in the Information Technology sector. It helps in developing the know-how process in India in terms of enhancing the technological advancement in India.
5. **Linkages and spill over to domestic firms:** Various foreign firms are now occupying a position in the Indian market through Joint Ventures and collaboration concerns. The maximum amount of the profits gained by the foreign firms through these joint ventures is spent on the Indian market.

4.7.6 Prohibited Sectors for FDI

1. Gambling and betting
2. Lottery Business
3. Atomic Energy
4. Retail Trading
5. Agricultural or plantation activities of Agriculture

(excluding Floriculture, Horticulture, Development of Seeds, Animal Husbandry, and Cultivation of Vegetables, Mushrooms etc., under controlled conditions and services related to agro and allied sectors) and Plantations other than Tea Plantations)

4.8 FOREIGN INSTITUTIONAL INVESTOR

An investor or investment fund that is from or registered in a country outside of the one in which it is currently investing.

Institutional investors include

- hedge funds,
- insurance companies,
- Pension funds and mutual funds.

4.8.1 Parameters on which SEBI decides FII applicants' eligibility

- Applicant's track record, professional competence, financial soundness, experience,
- General reputation of fairness and integrity. (The applicant should have been in existence for at least one year)
- whether the applicant is registered with and regulated by an appropriate Foreign Regulatory Authority in the same capacity in which the application is filed with SEBI
- Whether the applicant is a fit & proper person.

4.8.2 Advantages of FII

- Enhanced flows of equity capital.
- FIIs have a greater appetite for equity than debt in their asset structure. The opening up the economy to FIIs has been in line with the accepted preference for non-debt creating foreign inflows over foreign debt. Enhanced flow of equity capital helps improve capital structures and contributes towards building the investment gap.
- Managing uncertainty and controlling risks.
- FII inflows help in financial innovation and development of hedging instruments. Also, it not only enhances competition in financial markets, but also improves the alignment of asset prices to fundamentals.
- Improving capital markets.

- FIIs as professional bodies of asset managers and financial analysts enhance competition and efficiency of financial markets.
- Equity market development aids economic development
- By increasing the availability of riskier long term capital for projects, and increasing firms' incentives to provide more information about their operations, FIIs can help in the process of economic development.
- Improved corporate governance.
- FIIs constitute professional bodies of asset managers and financial analysts, who, by contributing to better understanding of firms' operations, improve corporate governance. Bad corporate governance makes equity finance a costly option. Also, institutionalization increases dividend payouts, and enhances productivity growth.

4.8.3 Disadvantages of FII

- **Problems of Inflation:** Huge amounts of FII fund inflow into the country creates a lot of demand for rupee, and the RBI pumps the amount of Rupee in the market as a result of demand created.
- **Problems for small investor**: The FIIs profit from investing in emerging financial stock markets. If the cap on FII is high then they can bring in huge amounts of funds in the country's stock markets and thus have great influence on the way the stock markets behaves, going up or down. The FII buying pushes the stocks up and their selling shows the stock market the downward path. This creates problems for the small retail investor, whose fortunes get driven by the actions of the large FIIs.
- **Adverse impact on Exports**: FII flows leading to appreciation of the currency may lead to the exports industry becoming uncompetitive due to the appreciation of the rupee.
- **Hot Money:** "Hot money" refers to funds that are controlled by investors who actively seek short-term returns. These investors scan the market for short-term, high interest rate investment opportunities. "Hot money" can have economic and financial repercussions on countries and banks. When money is injected into a country, the exchange rate for the country gaining the money strengthens, while the exchange rate for the country losing the money weakens. If money is withdrawn on short notice, the banking institution will experience a shortage of funds.

4.9 MULTINATIONAL CORPORATIONS

MNC's are huge industrial organizations which extend their industrial and marketing operations through a network of their branches or their Majority Owned Foreign Affiliates.

According to an ILO Report, "the essential nature of multinational enterprises lies in the fact that its managerial headquarters are located in one country (home country) while enterprises carries out operations in number of other countries as well (Host Countries).

MNC's are also known as Transnational Corporation (TNC's).

What's in a Name

There is a debate about what to call a company, whose business ranges across national borders, tying together home and host countries through corporate policies and practices. Here are some of the terms used to describe these companies.

Transnational Corporation (TNC)

Because companies "transcend" or operate across national borders, some experts prefer the term transnational corporation, or TNC. The United Nations favour this term and has created a research centre for the study of Transnational Corporations.

Multinational Corporation (MNC)

The fact that companies operate in multiple countries has led some experts to adopt the term Multinational Corporation, or MNC. This term is very popular in the business press and in textbooks. It seems to be the most generic name to describe corporations operating around the world.

Multinational Enterprise (MNE)

Because some of the international giants are state-owned enterprise, rather than corporations, the term multinational enterprise, or MNE, has entered the vocabulary of international trade.

4.9.1 Organization of Multinational Corporations

Multinational company can organize its operations in different countries through either of the following alternatives:

- Branches
- Subsidiaries
- Joint Ventures Companies
- Franchise Holders

4.9.2 Reasons for the Growth of MNC's

1. Expansion of market territory.
2. Marketing superiorities.
3. Financial Superiorities.
4. Technological Superiorities.
5. Product Innovations.

4.9.3 Merits of MNC's

The important arguments in favour of MNC's are given below–

MNC's help the host countries in following ways–

1. MNC's help to increases the investment level & thereby the income & employment in host country.
2. The transnational corporations have become vehicles for the transfer technology, especially to developing countries.
3. They also kind a managerial revolution in host countries through professional management and employment of highly sophisticated management techniques.
4. The MNCs enable that host countries to increases their exports & decreases their import requirements.
5. They work to equalize cost of factors of production around the world.
6. MNC's provide and efficient means of integrating national economies.
7. The enormous resources of multinational enterprises enable them to have very efficient research & development systems. Thus, they make a commendable contribution to inventions & innovations.
8. MNC's also stimulate domestic enterprise because to support their own operations, the MNC's may encourage & assist domestic suppliers.
9. MNC's help to increase competition & break domestic monopolies.

4.9.4 Demerits of MNC's

1. MNC's may destroy competition & acquire monopoly powers.
2. The transfer pricing enables MNC's to avoid taxes by manipulating prices on intra-company transactions.
3. Through their power and flexibility, MNC's can evade national economic autonomy & control, and their activities may be inimical to national income interests of particular countries.
4. MNCs retard growth of employment in home country.
5. MNCs technology is designed for world-wide Profit maximization, not the development needs of poor countries. In general, it is asserted, the imported technologies are not adapted to...
   - Consumption needs
   - Size of domestic markets
   - Resource availabilities
   - Stage of development of many of developing countries.

4.9.5 Multinationals in India

Comparatively very little foreign investment has taken place in India due to several reasons, some multinationals, Coca Cola and IBM, even left India in late 1970s as the government conditions were unacceptable to them.

A Common criticism against MNC's is that they tend to invest in low priority & high profit sectors in developing countries, ignoring national priorities. However high technology and heavy investment sectors of national importance & export sectors. Firms which had been established non-priority areas prior to implementation of this policy have however been allowed to continue in those sectors.

It is not a right approach to estimate the net impact of multinationals on foreign exchange reserves by taking net foreign exchange outflow or inflow. If a multinational is operating in an import substitution industry, the net effect in foreign exchange reserves could be favourable even if there is net foreign exchange outflow of company.

Indian MNCs (List of Acquires of Firms Abroad)

- Tata motors to takeover Daewoo in South Korea for $118 million
- Ambanis to takeover flag international for $211 million
- Ranbaxy to takeover RPG Aventis a France based firm
- Wockhardt acquired CP pharmaceutical and Wallis Laboratories --both of Britain
- Hindalco took over mount garden and Nifty--copper mines in Australia
- Sundaram Fasteners has acquired Dana spicer Europe, the British arm of an MNC.
- Amtek Auto has acquired the GWK group in the UK
- Kirloskar Brothers took over SPP pumps, UK

Multiple Choice Questions

1. In common parlance business refers to buying and selling of ....
   (a) Party (b) Unit
   (c) Goods & services (d) Team
2. Modern business covers a complex field of industry and .... which involve activities related to both production and distribution–
   (a) Trade (b) Union
   (b) Community (d) Commerce
3. Oligopolistic business is characterized by small number of firms selling a .... product–
   (a) Homogenous (b) Hetrogenous
   (c) Interdependent (d) Complimentary
4. Environment by definitions is something external to an individual or an..........
   (a) Community (b) Organization
   (c) Team (d) Group
5. Value system goals and objective, management structure, relationship among the various constituents, physical assets, technological capabilities and human, financial and marketing resources make the ....environment of business.
   (a) Hetrogenous (b) Internal
   (c) Enternal (d) Political
6. External environment can be classified into two as Macro and .... Enviroment.
   (a) Micro (b) Technological
   (c) Socio-cultural (d) Political

7. Macro environment, comprises large societal and physical forces which affect the company and also the players in the company's ....enviroment.
   (a) Macro (b) Micro
   (c) Internal (d) Political & legal
8. Buffering, leveling, anticipation.........dominating and changing technique can be used to cope with the changing environment.
   (a) Rationing (b) Interaction
   (c) Positioning (d) Segmenting
9. ....is the process through which an organization monitors and comprehends various environmental forces so as to determine the opportunities and threats that lie ahead.
   (a) Appraisal (b) Environmental Analysis
   (c) Forecasting (d) Controlling
10. Environmental factors and assessed in terms of their impact on the organization and this called.........
    (a) Diagnosis (b) Monitoring
    (c) Forecasting (d) Regulating
11. ....is a follow up and deeper analysis of relevant environmental forces identified through scanning.
    (a) Up dating (b) Scanning
    (c) Forecasting (d) Monitoring
12. SWOT stands for strength, weakness .... & threats.
    (a) Opportunity (b) Organization
    (c) Out come (d) Out standing
13. ETOP stands for .... Environmental threats and opportunities profile.
    (a) Environmental (b) Economics
    (c) Ecological (d) Ethics
14. Approaches to Environmental analysis are classified as
    (a) Systematic (b) Adhoc
    (c) Processed (d) Proposal
15. Which of the following is influenced by monetary policy.
    (a) Cost and availability of credit, money
    (b) Excess supply
    (c) Opportunities and threats
    (d) Strength and weakness of oragnistion

16. Which policy refers to the process of shaping taxation and public expenditure in order to damped the swings of the business cycle and to contribute to rapid economic growth and high employment and stable price.
    (a) Monetary (b) Fiscal
    (c) RBI policy (d) Strategic policy
17. Which of the following constitute defines property and business organization, laws of contracts and bankruptcy, mutual obligations of labour and management and a multitude of laws and regulations constraining the way business are carried out.
    (a) Legal Environmental (b) Technological Environmental
    (c) Social Environment (d) Cultural Environment
18. Which of the following is not included in social environment.
    (a) Ethical Environment (b) Political Environment
    (c) Technological Environment (d) Socio-cultural Environment
19. Which of the following consists of the exchange of goods and services between persons or organization operating in two or more countries.
    (a) Home trade (b) International trade
    (c) Import trade (d) Export trade
20. In India the present rate is:
    (a) 12% (b) 11%
    (c) 10% (d) 6%
21. Identify the correct statement:
    (a) The target for the growth rate as laid down in the Tenth Plan was 5.6 per cent per annum
    (b) The rate of domestic savings by the end of the Tenth Plan should be around 30 per cent of GDP.
    (c) Rate of investment will be 28.4 per cent in Tenth Plan.
    (d) The sector which has been given maximum boost in Tenth plan is Industry.
22. The period of the Tenth Plan is:
    (a) 1997-2003 (b) 2002-2007
    (c) 2001-2005 (d) None of the these
23. The target of Tenth Plan is to reduce poverty. Ratio by 5 percentage points by:
    (a) 2005 (b) 2006
    (c) 2007 (d) 2008
24. The Out by for Industry and mixrols in Tenth Plan is:
    (a) 58,939 corers (b) 85.940 corers

(c) 94, 532 cores (d) None of these

25. First industrial policy of free India was announced in:
    (a) 1991 (b) 2001
    (c) 1947 (d) 1948
26. Which industrial policy move towards Globalization and privatization of Indian economy?
    (a) 1957 (b) 2004
    (c) 1991 (d) 1970
27. MRTP Act was passed in:
    (a) 1969 (b) 1955
    (c) 1972 (d) 1999
28. IDRA was established in:
    (a) November 1950 (b) December 1949
    (c) March 1949 (d) October 1951
29. New licensing policy came into existence in the year:
    (a) 1990 (b) 1991
    (c) 1992 (d) 1993
30. When Competition Act was enforced?
    (a) 1998 (b) 1999
    (c) 2000 (d) 2001
31. The monetary policy, as pursued by the Reserved Bank of India, can be apply summed up in the phrase:
    (a) Neural mony (b) Cheap money
    (c) Dear money (d) Controlled monetary expansion
32. Open market operations refer to:
    (a) Purchase and sale of Government securities by the Reserve Bank
    (b) Borrowing by scheduled banks from the Reserve Bank
    (c) Lending by commercial banks to industry and trade
    (d) Deposit mobilization
33. The share of the developed countries in the world trade is:
    (a) 60% (b) 80%
    (c) 75% (d) 50%
34. The rate of growth in world trade had always been higher than the growth in:
    (a) World production (b) World economy
    (c) Both (a) and (b) (d) None of these

35. The factors of the business which can be controlled are called:
    (a) Micro Environment (b) Macro Environment
    (c) Internal Environment (d) None of these
36. The company's immediate environment that affect the performance of the company is called:
    (a) Internal Environmental (b) External Environmental
    (c) Micro Environment (d) None of these
37. Which of the following is not included in the micro environment?
    (a) Suppliers (b) Customers
    (c) Public (d) Producers
38. Which of the following statement is not true?
    (a) Macro forces are uncontrollable
    (b) Business environment is multificed
    (c) Every aspects of business depends upon natural environment
    (d) India is a closed economy
39. A major favourable situation in the firms's environment is called:
    (a) Strength (b) Opportunity
    (c) Resource (d) None of these
40. Opportunities and threats are related to:
    (a) External environment (b) Internal environment
    (c) Micro environment (d) None of these
41. Which of the following statement is not true?
    (a) SWOT is subjective
    (b) Strength and weaknesses are external factors
    (c) A firm's strengths are its resources
    (d) Environment analysis is a step toward corporate planning
42. The first National Income in India was estimated by:
    (a) Dada Bhai Naurozi (b) Prof. Pigou
    (c) Prnf. Marshall (d) None of these
43. The first chairman of National Income Committee of India was:
    (a) Mahalanobis (b) Prof. Shirras
    (c) Prof. Ghosh (d) None of these

44. For international comparisons to measure the level of economic well-being in different counties, we make use data relating to:
   (a) Money national income (b) Real per capita income
   (c) Money per capita income (d) Real national income
45. Region-wise, among the following, the state at a bottom of the ladder of per cpita income is
   (a) Jammu & Kashmir (b) U.P.
   (c) Punjab (d) Bihar
46. The state, among the following, at the top of the ladder of per capita income is:
   (a) Karnataka (b) Kerala
   (c) Andhra Pradesh (d) Goa
47. Per capita income at current prices has increased at a slower rate than the national income at current prices. This is indicative of fact than:
   (a) Distribution of national income has been getting to be more uneven so that poor have been becoming poorer and the rich, richer
   (b) Population has been rising at a faster rate than the growth of national income
   (c) Wholesale price index had been rising at a faster rate than the growth of population
   (d) None of these
48. The increase in national income as a measure for economic growth is in:
   (a) Real terms (b) Money terms
   (c) Both money and real terms (d) None of these
49. Industrial development in India has been retarded due to:
   (a) Power shortage (b) Labour unrest
   (c) Capital deficiency (d) All of the above
50. The Industrial Policy Resolution, 1956 had the provision for:
   (a) Classification of Industries into 3 schedules
   (b) Fair and non-discriminatory treatment for the private sector
   (c) Encouraging cottage and small scale industries
   (d) All the above
51. The new Industrial Policy has been in operation since:
   (a) May 25, 1991 (b) August 26, 1991
   (c) July 24, 1991 (d) December 22, 1991
52. The New Industrial Policy states that the stick and loss in loss incurring public enterprises should be referred to the:
   (a) SBI (b) FERA

(c) BIFR (d) RBI

53. Which Industrial Policy converted MRTP Act into a toothless Act?
    (a) 1956 (b) 1980
    (c) 1948 (d) 1991
54. Fiscal policy is associated with:
    (a) Banking Companies Act, 1949 (b) Companies Act, 1956
    (c) Income Tax Act, 1961 (d) Foreign Trade and Regulation Act, 1992
55. Which is not an objective of fiscal policy?
    (a) Reducing inequalities of Income (b) Controlling Inequalities of Income
    (c) Accelerating the rate of Investment (d) Achieving full employment
56. Fiscal deficit means:
    (a) Relying on foreign Aid
    (b) Spending by borrowing from abroad
    (c) Npt spending enough to ensure development
    (d) Spending in exces of revenue
57. Fiscal Policy in India has an objective of:
    (a) Management of Public debt (b) Regression Taxation
    (c) Establishment of welfare state (d) All of these
58. Fiscal policy is related to:
    (a) Issue of Currency (b) Credit creation
    (c) Public revenue and (d) All these expenditure
59. The Reserve Bank of India was established on ....under the RBI Act, 1934:
    (a) 21 st April, 1935 (b) 11th April, 1934
    (c) Ist April, 1935 (d) 11th April 1935
60. Identify the correct statement
    (a) According to Myrdal the foreign trade as promoted industrial development in poor countries.
    (b) International trade serves as a vehicle for the dissemination effect.
    (c) Income elasticity of demand for agriculture production is high in poor countires
    (d) Foreign trade does not have any demonstration effect.
61. The head office of RBI is situated at:
    (a) Delhi (b) Kolkata
    (c) Bangalore (d) Mumbai

62. The Reserve Bank of India was nationalized in:

(a) 1949 (b) 1946

(c) 1948 (d) 1950

63.The increase in the value of world exports has been due to:

(a) An increase in export prices

(b) An increase in the volume of exports

(c) Both (a) and (b)

(d) None of these

64. The Objectives of Reserve Bank includes:

(a) To regulate the issue of currency in India

(b) To maintain and manage stability in the country

(c) To establish monetary stability in the country

(d) To develop the financial structure nf the county on the basis of the national economics social objectives a policies.

(e) All the above

65. As a bankers bank the RRT has the authority of allow the banks:

(a) To issue currency notes

(b) To control the volume of reserves of bank

(c) To allow every bank to frame its own policies for classification of their assets.

66. As a bankers to the Government RBI provides to the Government:

(a) Ways and means advances (b) Bill of exchange

(c) Clean notes (d) Supervision on investments

Answers

1. (c)	**2.** (d)	**3.** (d)	**4.** (b)	**5.** (b)	**6.** (a)	**7.** (b)	**8.** (a)	**9.** (b)	**10.** (a)
11. (d)	**12.** (a)	**13.** (a)	**14.** (c)	**15.** (a)	**16.** (b)	**17.** (a)	**18.** (b)	**19.** (b)	**20.** (a)
21. (c)	**22.** (b)	**23.** (c)	**24.** (a)	**25.** (d)	**26.** (c)	**27.** (a)	**28.** (d)	**29.** (b)	**30.** (c)
31. (d)	**32.** (a)	**33.** (c)	**34.** (a)	**35.** (c)	**36.** (c)	**37.** (d)	**38.** (d)	**39.** (b)	**40.** (a)
41. (b)	**42.** (a)	**43.** (a)	**44.** (c)	**45.** (d)	**46.** (d)	**47.** (d)	**48.** (a)	**49.** (d)	**50.** (d)
51. (c)	**52.** (c)	**53.** (d)	**54.** (c)	**55.** (b)	**56.** (d)	**57.** (c)	**58.** (c)	**59.** (c)	**60.** (b)
61. (d)	**62.** (a)	**63.** (c)	**64.** (d)	**65.** (b)	**66.** (a)				

Index

A

Adaptive 19
Adhoc Approach 6
Agriculture sector 36
Arthur M. Weimer 1
Automated Teller Machine (ATM) 76

B

Banking Sector Reforms 71
Bayard O. Wheeler 1
Bombay 31
Bombay Stock Exchange 59
Business Environment 1

C

Capital Market 60, 61
Capital Market Structure 62
Capitalism 11
Capitalism Economy 10, 11
Categorization of industries 41
Central Bank 70, 71
Co-existence of public and private sector 13
Commercial Paper 65
Consumer Protection 82
Consumer Protection Act 1986 29
Consumer Rights 81
Consumerism 81
Continuous Process 4
Culture Environment 19
Culture on business 19

D

Debt Definition 60
Def Harry G. Johnson 50
Democracy 15
Depository System in India 66
Derivatives 68, 69
Dictatorship 15
Direct Control 16

Domestication 18

E

E-Banking 75
Economic Roles 16
Eighth Plan (1992-97) 34
Employment 48
Environmental Analysis 3
Environmental Scanning 3
EQUALITY 16, 40
Equity Definition 60
EXIM Policy 92, 93, 98
Existence of central plan 14
Existence of competition 13
Exploratory Process 4
Export 48
Expropriation 18
External Environment 8

F

Fifth Plan (1974-79) 33
Financial Sector Reform in India 73
Firm's Strength 2
First Plan (1951-56) 32
Fiscal Policy 53, 54, 55
forecasting process 4
Foreign Direct Investment 100
Foreign Exchange Management Act, 1999 26
Fourth Plan (1969-74) 33
FRATERNITY 16, 40
Freedom of occupation 14
Freedom on Consumption 13
Freedom to save and invest 13

G

Global Environment 23
Globalisation 88
Government Borrowing 55
Government Controls 15
Government Securities Market 63
groundwork for scanning 3

H

Hedger 68

I

Image Building 2
Indian Capital Market 61
Indian Experience of E-banking 79
Indirect Control 16
Industrial Policy 37, 38
Industrial Policy Resolution of 1948 38
Industrial Policy Resolution of 1956 40
Industrial Policy Resolution of 1991 44
Industrial Policy resolution of December 23, 1977 43
Industrial Policy Resolution of February 2, 1973 43
Industrial Policy Resolution of July 1980 44
Industrial Securities Market 62
Inequitable distribution of Income 14
information climate 5
Internal Environment 7
Internet Banking 76
Investment Limits 47

J

John Dewey 19
JUSTICE 16, 40

K

KISCH AND ELKIN 70

L

Learned 19
Learning 2
LIBERTY 16, 40
Long-term Loans Market 63

M

Macroeconomic Goals 54
Management Decision Making 22
Market Mechanism 14
Micro Environment 8
Mixed Economy 13
Mixed sector 39
Monetary Policy 50, 51, 52, 53
Money Market 63, 64
Monopolistic Trade Practice 25
MRTP Act 24, 25
Multinational Corporations 110

N

Narasimhan Committee 73
National Stock Exchange of India 60
New Economic Policy-1991 85
New Issue Market 62
Ninth Plan (1997-2002) 34
Non-programmed decisions 22

O

Opportunities 2, 49

P

People's Plan 31
Planning 32
Political Environment 15
Political Risks of Global Business 17
Primary Sources 7
Problems of SSI 49
Processed-Form Approach 6
Programmed decisions 22
Public Expenditure 55

R

R G HAWTREY 70
Refining the scanning 4
Reserve Bank of India 70
Restrictive Trade Practice 25
Review of Five Year Plans 32

S

SEBI 29
Second Plan (1956-61) 32
Secondary Market 63
Secondary Sources 7
Securities Contracts (Regulation) Act 1956 56
Security Definition 60
Seventh Plan (1985-90) 34
Shared 19
Shri M N Roy 31
Sixth Plan (1980-85) 33

Small-Scale Industry 47
Smart Card 77
Social Environment 18
Social Responsibility of Business 83
Socialism Economy 12
"Socialistic Pattern of Society" 40
Socio-cultural Environment 18
Sri M.Visvesvaraya 31
Stock Exchange 55, 56, 57, 58
Swot 3
Systematic Approach 6

T

Technological Environment in India 22
Tele Banking 77
Tenth Plan (2002-07) 35
Third Plan (1961-66) 33
Threats 2
Tran generational 19

V

Value system 7

W

Weakness 2